Disney's
WONDERFUL WORLD OF KNOWLEDGE

Disney's

Wonderful World of Knowledge

THE DANBURY PRESS

THE DANBURY PRESS

a division of Grolier Enterprises, Inc.

ROBERT B. CLARKE   *Publisher*

THE STONEHOUSE PRESS   *Production Supervision*

ARNOLDO MONDADORI EDITORE

MARIO GENTILINI   *Editor-in-Chief*

ELISA PENNA   *Supervising Editor*

GIOVAN BATTISTA CARPI   *Illustrators*
CLAUDIO MAZZOLI

GUIDO MARTINA   *Author*

CONTENTS

THE FOUR MUSKETEERS

Have any of you boys and girls read a book called *The Three Musketeers?* If you have you might remember that there were really four and not three musketeers. Our story is something like that. There are four and not three main characters—although at first it may not seem so. The fourth character is a surprise.

But I don't want to confuse you. So let me start by introducing the first three characters. Actually the leader of the group is so famous he needs no introduction. He's the one and only Donald Duck. Donald is going to be the "pilot" on this whirlwind flight around the globe. One of his two copilots is a champion chatterbox from Brazil—a parrot named José Carioca. The other is Panchito, the Mexican jumping bean, who fancies himself as brave and cocky as a bullfighter.

The fourth character is the airplane our heroes are going to fly. But you will have to wait a bit longer to find out about that. Anyway, our story begins one afternoon when Donald took José and Panchito on a tour of fabulous Disneyland, the world's capital of fun. They ended their tour at an outdoor ice-cream parlor, where they chatted about old times. Here is what went on that day. . . .

THE GAY CABALLEROS

"It sure is nice to get together again after all these years," exclaimed José Carioca, happily digging into a hot fudge sundae.

"Yes, indeed," said Donald, gulping down the remains of a banana split. "I can still remember the great time we had together traveling through Latin America. What a trip that was!"

"Was it ever," added little Panchito, who could hardly be seen behind a huge ice cream soda. "They called us the 'Three Caballeros.' What a time we had."

"I wonder why we didn't travel anymore after that," José said.

Donald shook his head sadly. "It's really a shame, especially since there are so many wonderful and exciting places to visit all over the world. Just think, there are whole continents out there waiting for us."

An astronaut's view of the planet Earth. This picture was taken from the Apollo 11 spacecraft. The dark areas in the photograph are the continents; the lighter areas are the oceans.

9

"Continents? What are continents?" Panchito asked.

José Carioca laughed smugly. "You mean you don't know what continents are?"

"All right, if you're so smart, what are they?" Panchito snorted.

"Why, they are . . . uh . . . they are. . . . Come to think of it, I'm not quite sure."

"Let me tell you then," said Donald. "We divide our planet into a number of great landmasses. These large divisions of land are called continents. For example, Africa is a continent."

"You sure are a smart one, Donald," Panchito commented.

Each year millions of visitors from all over the world come to Disneyland, the fabulous amusement park in southern California.
Below: The world of tomorrow is represented by this model of an Apollo rocket.

"Since you know so much," snapped José, "tell us how many continents there are."

"That's easy," Donald replied. "There are seven altogether. But, of course, if we consider North America and South America as one continent, there are just six. And, if we combine Europe and Asia into a single continent called Eurasia, there are only five. And furthermore, if. . . ."

At that point, José and Panchito called for him to stop. "Wait a minute, Donald, you're getting us all mixed up. That's not fair!"

Donald laughed and laughed. "Okay, don't get excited fellows. I was just having a little fun. Actually geographers will tell you that there are seven continents. They are North America, South America, Europe, Asia, Africa, Australia, and Antarctica. Now that's simple enough isn't it?"

"It sure is, now that you have explained it to us," José agreed. "But tell me, how do you happen to know so much about a subject like continents?"

Above: For a journey into the past, the visitor can stroll through "Old America," which features booming brass bands and Dixieland jazz.

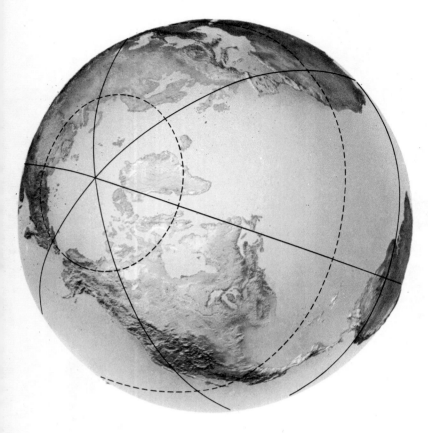

Oceans and seas cover nearly three fourths of the surface of the globe, as illustrated above. The major oceans are the Pacific and the Atlantic.

Donald looked around to see if anyone was listening. Then he told them. "I'm going to let you boys in on a little secret. I've decided to enter a quiz show to try to win some of those wonderful prizes. The subject I've picked is geography, and I've been reading up on it these last few weeks."

"Gosh, that's terrific Donald," José commented. "But I've always believed that the best way to learn about a place is to visit it yourself. Now if you were to go to all of those countries and—what's that word? Oh, yes—continents, you would certainly learn much more about geography. Then you would be a cinch to beat all the other quiz show contestants."

Donald broke into a wide grin. "That's a great idea, José. A trip around the world—from one continent to another."

"Oh, boy, Panchito exclaimed, jumping up and down so that his tiny sombrero nearly fell off his head. "That means we can travel together again—just like old times."

Suddenly José became downcast. "I just thought of something, fellows. We don't have enough money for airplane tickets."

"Don't worry about that," Donald said cheerily. "I know how we can do it without spending a cent."

"Travel without paying for our transportation!" Panchito said in amazement. "But how is that possible?"

Donald didn't answer immediately. He had his eyes fixed on something flying overhead. It was a large, round object, and it seemed to have two flapping wings.

Donald pointed to the sky. "There's our airplane, boys—our old friend Dumbo, the flying elephant."

And a moment later, with a bounce and a jolt, Dumbo landed beside them.

Our fourth character has arrived!

Our characters will be traveling in an orbit around the Earth from Disneyland, California, to Disney World, Florida—a distance of about 25,000 miles.

COME FLY WITH ME

Playfully wagging his trunk, Dumbo called out, "Hello, fellows, what's up?"

Donald quickly filled him in on the details of their plan to use him as their airplane for a flight around the world. Now, Dumbo is a goodnatured, agreeable elephant, but he seemed a little taken aback by the idea.

"My goodness," he declared. "I've been on some long trips in my time, but to fly around the world . . . Gee, I don't know if I can manage that. We might get lost."

"Nonsense," said Donald firmly. "It's really very simple. All we have to do is keep flying in one direction. Since the earth is round, we will eventually come back to where we started."

"It's as easy as eating a tortilla," Panchito said with a wide grin.

"Exactly," Donald agreed. "What do you say, Dumbo, old friend? I know you're the right elephant for this job."

Dumbo thought for a moment. Then his ears began to flap excitedly. "I suppose I can't let you fellows down, especially since you have such confidence in me. Okay, I'll do it!"

"Hooray for Dumbo!" they all yelled together, patting his trunk.

"Now that's settled," Donald declared. "All we have to do is figure out a flight plan."

"You're the geography expert, Donald," José said. "You decide."

Donald took out his pocket encyclopedia, which he always carries with him. "Hmm, let me see," he mumbled as he skimmed through the book. "I have it! Let's start with the oldest part of the world. The first civilizations were in Asia—so we'll begin in the exotic lands of the East."

"And then what, Donald?" Panchito asked breathlessly.

"We'll make our way through Africa and Europe and then go across to the youngest part of our globe—the New

A bird's-eye view of Los Angeles, the largest city in California. Just south of Los Angeles, in Anaheim, is Disneyland—from where we begin our world tour.

World of the Americas."

"It sounds great," commented Dumbo. "I just hope my ears hold out."

"Let's stop talking and get on with it," said José.

"Which way do I go?" asked Dumbo, as the others climbed onto his back.

Donald pointed west across the Pacific. "That's the way to the eastern lands."

José was mystified. "You mean we're going to travel west to get to the East?"

"Of course," replied Donald. "Don't you remember how Columbus sailed west to reach the East, because he knew the earth was round? We're going to follow in his footsteps. Okay, Dumbo, let's take off!"

A moment later, with his passengers clinging to his back, Dumbo went soaring into the air.

"Yippee, we're off!" they yelled.

Flap, flap, flap went Dumbo's long ears as the blue-green waters of the Pacific began to pass below them. . . .

15

ON LAND
AND SEA

While our three brave heroes are still flying, let's sit down together and get some important ideas clear in our heads.

Donald was right when he said that if you kept traveling around the earth in the same direction you would end up at the point where you started your trip. This is because the earth is round. Well, not exactly round. Pear-shaped is a better way to describe it. You see, the earth is slightly flattened at the North and South poles. It bulges out a bit around the middle, or equator, as the line exactly half way between the two poles is called. Recently measurements made from a space satellite showed that there were two depressions that you might call "dimples" in the northern hemisphere.

Keep your eye on that pear, but remember it's not time to eat yet! Instead, let's take a look at the story of how long it took men to get this pear-shaped view of their planet.

Here's a surprise! Some Greeks of the 6th century B.C. guessed (almost cor-

rectly as it turned out) that the earth was round. They passed this vital information along to the Romans. But then in the upheavals and wars that shook Europe between the 5th and 12th centuries A.D., this very important fact was lost or forgotten.

As a result the Europeans of the Middle Ages thought that the world was made up of only four landmasses, or continents. They were Europe, Africa, Asia, and a mysterious blob of land they called *Terra Incognita*, which means "unknown land" in Latin. Since our ancestors had never seen this unknown place, they just guessed it was located in the Southern Hemisphere. Centuries later when Australia was discovered by Europeans they called it *Terra Incognita Australis*—the "unknown southern Continent."

The map makers of medieval Europe were religious man and so they decided that the Holy City of Jerusalem (now in Israel) was located at the exact center of the world. Unfortunately this nice idea made medieval maps quite useless. The strange and incorrect maps had another exciting feature—dragons! The known world, those four continents we just talked about, were completely surrounded by a large and frightening ocean. Legends

Opposite page: An Egyptian zodiacal table from the Temple of Hathor in Dendera, now in the Louvre museum in Paris. Zodiacs were a way of showing the location of heavenly bodies in the sky. The word zodiac comes from the Greek word zoion *("animal"), as many constellations were named for animals.*

said that this vast ocean was filled with fire-breathing dragons and other monsters. Medieval maps included drawings of these creatures.

Naturally this misinformation discouraged all but the bravest men from even thinking about leaving their homes to look for new lands and seas. But, as you know, there were some men brave enough to overlook any danger. One of the most famous of these men was the 16th-century navigator, Ferdinand Magellan, who led the first voyage to sail around the globe. Magellan's historic trip made it clear to almost everybody that the earth was round. All those strange old maps were proved wrong. But even now new maps must be made as we continue to learn about the earth we live on.

Above: Alfred Lothar Wegener, the German geologist and explorer who developed the theory of continental drift. Left: A view of Greenland, the island that Wegener explored for his theory.

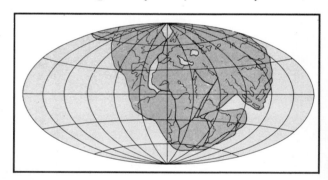

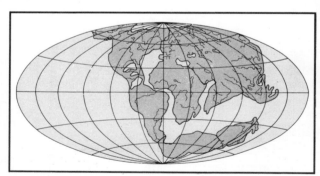

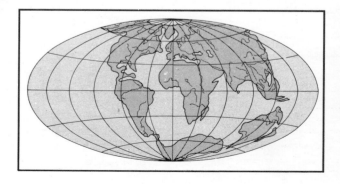

FACTS BENEATH YOUR FEET

Now here are some very big numbers to give you a more exact idea of your home planet's size.

Above: The village of Upernavik in Greenland. Greenland is a part of the Danish commonwealth. Below: An Eskimo girl gathers ice to be melted and used for fresh water.

Scientists say that if you could measure the surface area of earth you would find it to be about 197,272,000 square miles. The land area of earth covers only about 57,500,000 square miles. All the rest of the surface is covered by water. You can see that in some ways the old mapmakers were not so far from the truth—except, of course, for those fire-breathing dragons.

If you made one of those trips around the world that Donald was talking about you would have to cover about 24,890 miles at the equator. It would be a little shorter, however, if you could make the trip around the poles.

Now for a really huge number let's imagine that by some kind of magic you could put the earth on a scale. It would weigh about 6.6 sextillion tons. Wow! This is how it looks in numbers:

6,600,000,000,000,000,000,000.

WHAT IS A CONTINENT?

All those zeroes make me dizzy, so I thought it was time to go back to our three travelers.

Well, there they were, flying across the Pacific Ocean on Dumbo's back. Panchito looked as if he had seen enough ocean to last him for a long, long time. And there was Donald trying to make him feel better by reading to him from his handy encyclopedia.

"A continent is a large landmass," Donald read. "Each continent is shaped like a basin surrounded by mountains."

It looked to me as though Panchito and the others were not able to concentrate too well on what Donald was reading what with all those waves breaking below. But you know Donald—he went right on with his lecture from his encyclopedia, and it was a very important one, too.

A ROLL CALL OF THE CONTINENTS

"A roll call of the continents in order of their size," Donald read in his serious voice, "begins with Asia. Asia covers approximately 17,000,000 square miles and is the largest landmass in the world."

"The next largest continent is Africa, which covers about 11,703,860 square miles. North America, the third largest continent, covers about 9,160,000 square miles. Central and South America may be thought of as one continent. Together they cover approximately 7,084,455 square miles. Far to the south is the continent of Antarctica, which covers over 5,000,000 square and icy miles."

"Europe presents a problem to geographers because they still do not agree where Europe ends and Asia begins. Most people have decided that the Ural Mountains in the Soviet Union make a good

Below: The city of Alesund, Norway, an important fishing center. Opposite page: The fishing market in Bergen, Norway. Bergen, which is Norway's second largest city (the capital, Oslo, is the largest) is known as a major shipping center.

eastern border for Europe, when it is thought of as a separate continent. Europe, including the slice of the Soviet Union called European Russia, covers about 4,200,000 square miles."

"The smallest of all the continents is Australia, which covers only 2,967,910 square miles."

I could see that Donald had completely warmed up to his subject. He was about to go on with his learned explanations but it seemed to me down here that his companions were falling asleep. While they rested I thought it would be a good time for a look into the mystery of the supercontinent that disappeared.

THE SUPERCONTINENT THAT DISAPPEARED

Once upon a time, maybe 100,000,000 to 150,000,000 years ago, there may have been only one continent on our planet. As least that is what some earth scientists have decided after years of research.

If you look at the map of the world carefully you can see that the present-day continents could be thought of as the pieces of a gigantic jigsaw puzzle. In your imagination carefully put the pieces together to form the supercontinent. You will see that if you took away the South Atlantic Ocean and pressed South America and Africa together they would make one neatly fitting part of the puzzle. You could continue removing oceans and seas and putting the parts of the world together quite easily until you got to those two last pieces—Australia and Antarctica.

Where Australia and Antarctica once fitted in the supercontinent is a problem that confused scientists for a long time, too. Scientists recently have decided that the continents of Australia and Antarctica were once linked together. They may have split slowly off from the supercontinent and then separated from each other as recently as 40,000,000 years ago.

To really understand the idea of the

The Trevi Fountain, one of the most beautiful in Rome, Italy. Opposite page: A view of a town in the Ural Mountains, which separate Europe and Asia.

supercontinent we have to go much further back in time—more than 40,000,000, or even 150,000,000 years ago. You see it may have been about 4,500,000,000 (billion) years ago that the swirling masses of dust and gas broke off from the sun and condensed, forming our earth and the other planets. By about 3,000,000,000 (billion) years ago the earth's crust was well formed but beneath the crust the earth remained extremely hot. Gradually three separate layers formed. 23

They were the core, the mantle, and the surface. The mantle, which is about 1,800 miles thick now, lies between the core and the surface of the earth.

This mantle became covered very slowly with rocks. The heaviest rocks made a layer that completely covered the earth. The lighter rocks covered only about a quarter of the earth's surface. The cooling process went on and the earth's crust was formed from the heavy and light rocks. One mass of this rock formed the supercontinent that disappeared.

Scientists who believe that there was one supercontinent have named it Pa-nagea. The scientists who believe that there may have been two of these giant continents have named them Gondwana and Laurasia. Gondwana was made up of Australia, Africa, India, South America, and Malagasy. Laurasia was made up of parts of Europe, and North America, and Greenland.

Whether there were one or two of these supercontinents may never be known. But it is certain that the earth is still restless. The seven continents we know are still drifting on the surface of the earth at the rate of about an inch a year. This constant movement, plus the action of earthquakes and the explosion of volcanoes, makes it clear that our planet is still changing. If you could see a map of the world as it will look 1,000,000 years from now it might look as strange as a map drawn in the Middle Ages.

Statue of Liberty on Liberty Island in upper New York harbor, a gift from the people of France to the United States. It commemorates the French and American revolutions. Standing over 151 feet high, Miss Liberty, as the statue is sometimes called, is a symbol of the United States. A stairway makes it possible to climb to the top of the statue for a view of the port of New York (opposite page).

WATER, WATER EVERYWHERE

As long as our heroes have remained so nice and quiet we can switch the topic from continents to oceans.

Do you know where the word "ocean" comes from? Very, very old Greek legends told of the great river that surrounded the earth. This river was a god named Ocean. He married the nymph Tethys, and they had 3,000 sons. These sons were the 3,000 rivers that were thought to be on earth. Ocean and Tethys also had 3,000 daughters—the fountains and streams.

Later when man began to learn more about the earth, the large body of water surrounding the continents was called the Ocean Sea. It was only during the great period of exploration and discovery beginning in the 14th century that men began to give separate names to the different oceans and seas—names that we still use today.

The largest of the world's oceans is the Pacific. Early Asian travelers such as Marco Polo first brought word to Europe

ARCTIC

Perspective map by J. Donovan

of the great ocean that lay beyond that continent. But it was not until Vasco Nuñez de Balboa saw the Pacific from Panama, in 1513, that it was accepted as a separate body of water. Seven years later the explorer Magellan found the ocean so peaceful and free of storms that he named it the Pacific from the Latin *pace* for "peace."

The second largest ocean is the Atlan-

Above: The Bering Strait links the Arctic Ocean with the Bering Sea, which is an arm of the Pacific Ocean. Both the sea and the strait were named for Vitus Bering, the Danish explorer.

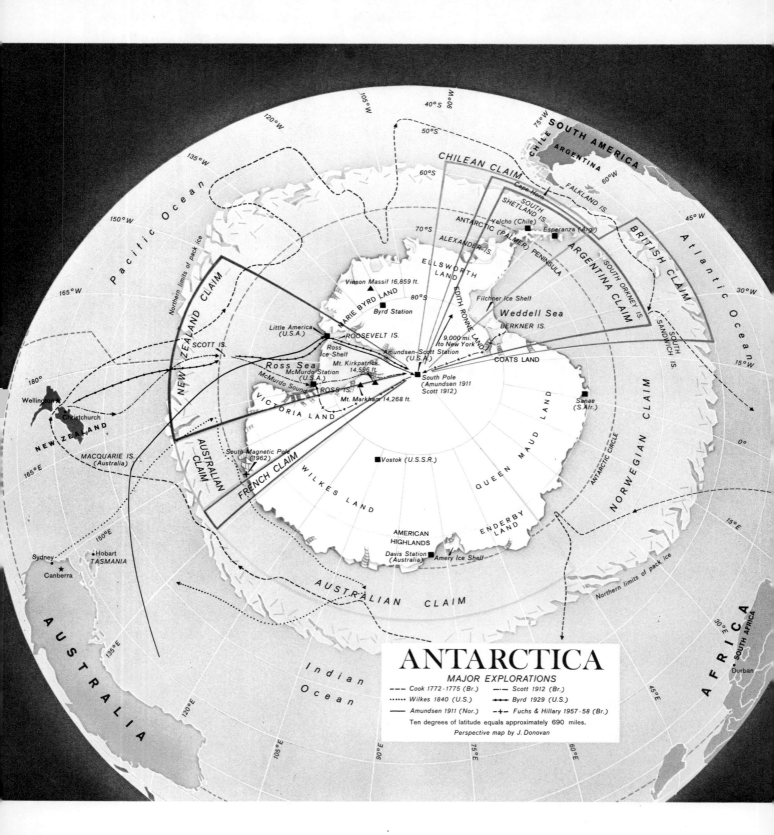

ANTARCTICA
MAJOR EXPLORATIONS

- – – – Cook 1772-1775 (Br.)
- ·········· Wilkes 1840 (U.S.)
- –––––– Amundsen 1911 (Nor.)
- –··–··– Scott 1912 (Br.)
- ←●→ Byrd 1929 (U.S.)
- –+–+– Fuchs & Hillary 1957-58 (Br.)

Ten degrees of latitude equals approximately 690 miles.

Perspective map by J. Donovan

CHILEAN CLAIM

BRITISH CLAIM

ARGENTINA CLAIM

NEW ZEALAND CLAIM

AUSTRALIAN CLAIM

FRENCH CLAIM

NORWEGIAN CLAIM

AUSTRALIAN CLAIM

SOUTH AMERICA

CHILE ARGENTINA

Cape Horn

FALKLAND IS.

SOUTH ORKNEY IS.

SOUTH SANDWICH IS.

SOUTH SHETLAND IS.

Yalcho (Chile)

Esperanza (Arg.)

ANTARCTIC (PALMER) PENINSULA

ALEXANDER IS.

ELLSWORTH LAND

EDITH RONNE LAND

Filchner Ice Shelf

Weddell Sea

BERKNER IS.

COATS LAND

Vinson Massif 16,859 ft.

MARIE BYRD LAND

Byrd Station

Little America (U.S.A.)

ROOSEVELT IS.

SCOTT IS.

Ross Ice Shelf

Ross Sea

Mt. Kirkpatrick 14,596 ft.

McMurdo Station (U.S.A.)

McMurdo Sound

ROSS IS.

Mt. Markham 14,268 ft.

9,000 mi. to New York

Amundsen-Scott Station (U.S.A.)

South Pole (Amundsen 1911 Scott 1912)

Sanae (S.Afr.)

VICTORIA LAND

South Magnetic Pole (1962)

WILKES LAND

QUEEN MAUD LAND

Vostok (U.S.S.R.)

ENDERBY LAND

AMERICAN HIGHLANDS

Davis Station (Australia)

Amery Ice Shelf

Northern limits of pack ice

Pacific Ocean

Atlantic Ocean

Indian Ocean

Wellington

Christchurch

NEW ZEALAND

MACQUARIE IS. (Australia)

Sydney

Hobart TASMANIA

Canberra

AUSTRALIA

AFRICA

SOUTH AFRICA

Durban

ANTARCTIC CIRCLE

Northern limits of pack ice

90°W
40°S
50°S
60°S
70°S
80°S
75°W
60°W
45°W
30°W
15°W
0°
15°E
30°E
45°E
60°E
75°E
90°E
105°E
120°E
135°E
150°E
165°E
180°
165°W
150°W
135°W
120°W
105°W

Above: Antarctica, the continent on which the South Pole is located, is desolate and sparsely inhabited. The only human beings who live there are scientific researchers. The best known inhabitants are the penguins.

tic, which also got its name in a strange way. According to another of those old legends, there was once a great island called Atlantis that grew very rich and important. Then, mysteriously, it disappeared. It was thought to be located in the region presently occupied by the Atlantic Ocean.

The Atlantic and the Pacific oceans are now linked by way of the Panama Canal. The Atlantic and the world's third largest ocean, the Indian Ocean, are connected by way of the Suez Canal across Egypt.

The Indian Ocean stretches from the coast of India to Antarctica and from Africa's east coast to Australia. It was once called the Indigo—Blue—Sea. The first European to explore it was Vasco da Gama in 1498.

Two other oceans—the Arctic and the Antarctic—are sometimes considered as separate bodies of water. Both of these seas are frozen or filled with pack ice for most of the year because of their position at the extreme northern and southern tips of the world.

There is some confusion about the word "seas." In the olden days people spoke of sailing the seven seas. But there are more than seven. You are correct if you call any large body of salty water a sea. This includes such inland seas as the Caspian, which is also ranked as the largest "lake" in the world.

HIGHS AND LOWS

While we are on the subject of biggest, we might as well go on to highest, lowest, and so on—before we get too confused about the difference between seas and oceans!

While we are still a little damp from the salty spray of the seas and oceans, I might as well tell you about the wettest place in the world. It is Mount Waialeale in Hawaii. Here the average annual rainfall is 460 inches. Far away in the Ata-

29

Left: A field at the foot of Mt. Everest, the highest peak in the Himalayas and in all the world. The word Himalayas means "home of the snows" in Sanskrit. Center: A view of Mt. Kilimanjaro, which is the highest peak in Africa. Coffee is grown on the lower slopes of the mountain.
Right: Mont Blanc, in the Alps, the highest peak in Western Europe. Its sharp outline shows that the mountain is still quite young because wind and weather have not softened its rocky face. A large glacier, the Mer de Glace, or "Sea of Ice," is on the mountain's western slope.

cama Desert in Chile so little rain falls that it cannot even be measured. It is, of course, the driest spot on earth.

If you are feeling very peppy you might like to think about climbing the highest mountain in the world. It is Mount Everest on the border between China and Nepal. The world's lowest point is the Dead Sea between Israel and Jordan and the deepest point is in the underwater Marianas Trench in the North Pacific Ocean. Feeling too warm? Then the place to go is Vostok in Antarctica, where the temperature once dipped to −127 degrees Fahrenheit. Or are you too cold? You might like a trip to Azizia, Libya, where it was once a scorching 136 degrees Fahrenheit.

PEOPLES OF THE WORLD

Now that you have been exposed to all these facts about your home planet, we can get back to our favorite topic—ourselves, or to put it properly, mankind.

Do you know how long man has lived on earth? No? You are in good company because even scientists are uncertain. Fossil bones that seem manlike have been dated to 14,000,000 years ago. But it is believed that our closer ancestors did not appear until about 2,500,000 years ago. As you can see that is a pretty short time in earth's history.

The population of the world grew fairly slowly at first, reaching about

250,000,000 by the beginning of the Christian Era. By 1970 there were 3,560,-000,000 (billion) people on earth and the population is expected to double by about the year 2000.

As you might guess this enormous number of people are spread out unevenly across the globe. The most heavily populated continent is Asia. The least populated continent is—you guessed it!—Antarctica, where there are more penguins than people. There are some scientists and technicians who have established research camps on the frozen continent, but they usually do not stay for long because of the frigid climate.

Speaking of climate we should say that except for extreme cold and extreme heat man has been able to adapt himself to live nearly anywhere on the globe. He has learned to build houses out of every possible material, from the ice used by the Eskimo for their igloos to the stone and

Among the ways scientists determine race is by skin color and the color and texture of hair. However, the important thing to remember is that all people, no matter where they live or how they look, share similar traits.

wood that we know best. Man has learned to make food plants grow nearly everywhere. He has tamed animals to help him and keep him company. Man has dug into the earth for coal, oil, metals, and minerals that could be used in his daily life. He has invented devices to make life easier and has worked to control diseases and prevent pain. We can all take pride in the things our ancestors have done to make the earth a home for man.

THE RACES OF MANKIND

A very, very important fact to remember on our journey across the continents with Donald, Panchito, José Carioca, and Dumbo is that people are more alike than they are different. All mankind has a common origin. As time passed and men settled in different parts of the world, they were naturally exposed to different kinds of climates, foods, diseases, and ex-

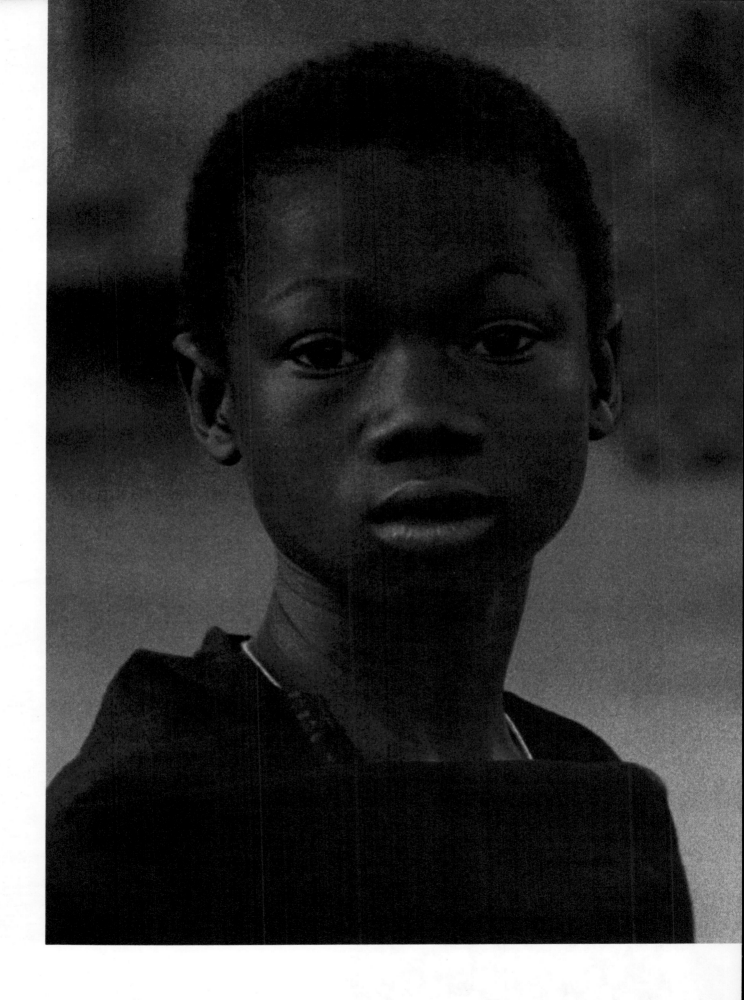

periences. Slowly, very slowly, differences began to develop in how men looked. But they were still all part of the same species, which is called *Homo sapiens*—"thinking man."

As a member of this species you know that the people of the world are sometimes divided into different races. This is done mainly to describe the differences in looks, body shape, and so on that have developed in people as they settled in widely separated parts of our planet.

The word race is used by scientists only to describe natural populations that have common blood groups as well as similar body build, skin color, and hair. Race has nothing to do with one's nationality, language, or religion.

Did you realize that the peoples of the earth live in over 100 different nations?

They speak over 3,000 different tongues, and worship in countless different ways. It is clear the old saying, "Variety is the spice of life," is true. Wherever you travel you will find people that are a lot like you and others that are quite a bit different. But whoever they are and wherever they live, they are really just like you—human beings living on the only inhabited planet in our solar system.

And now. . . .

Do you know what I heard? Panchito said "Cock-a-doodle-doo" in almost the same voice with which Columbus's lookout must have shouted "Land! Land!" when he sighted the New World. And that means that it's time for us to rejoin our three friends and Dumbo as his ears go Flap, Flap! for a landing on a continent full of adventures.

In contrast to the empty Antarctic landscape (below), huge crowds are often gathered in New York City (above and left). New York illustrates the problem of overpopulation that afflicts the earth. Scientists believe that this problem will become more serious in the years to come.

THE ANCIENT WORLD

Flap, Flap! Dumbo landed in an open space in the middle of a tropical forest.

"Here we are!," shouted Donald happily, jumping to the ground.

But Panchito took a look around and muttered puzzledly, "Who says so? This business of reaching the East by traveling west isn't really too convincing. Just where are we?"

"Suppose we ask at the information booth?," ventured José Carioca timidly.

Unfortunately there are no information booths in the jungle. But the place wasn't completely deserted because sounds could be heard coming from behind a bush.

"There's someone who can tell us," exclaimed Donald.

But as soon as that "someone" poked his head out of the bush, our three heroes jumped back onto Dumbo as quick as they could, and he flew up into a tall tree.

"A T-T-T-Tiger!," stuttered Panchito.

The temple of Jagganath, built in 1640 in Udaipur, India.

Dumbo asked, "Can tigers climb trees?"

"I don't know," answered Donald, "but I know that they live only in Asia, and that's proof that we've arrived."

Dumbo, meanwhile, was still casting fearful glances at the tiger. "Let's take off," he suggested. "That way we can get a better idea of what the land looks like."

Without waiting for an answer, Dumbo flew off, climbing several thousand feet into the air. From this height the cloudless sky was so clear that they could see all the way to the far horizon. Using their imagination, our travelers had the impression that they could see the Arctic Ocean to the north, the Pacific Ocean to the east, the Indian Ocean to the south, the Ural Mountains to the west, and, still farther west, the Black Sea, the strait of Bosporus, and the Mediterranean and the Red seas. These are the geographical boundaries of Asia.

Taking out his ever-present encyclopedia, Donald told the others:

"Asia has approximately 2,000,000,-000 (billion) people, well over half the world's total population. It is the largest continent. With its 17,000,000 square

ASIA

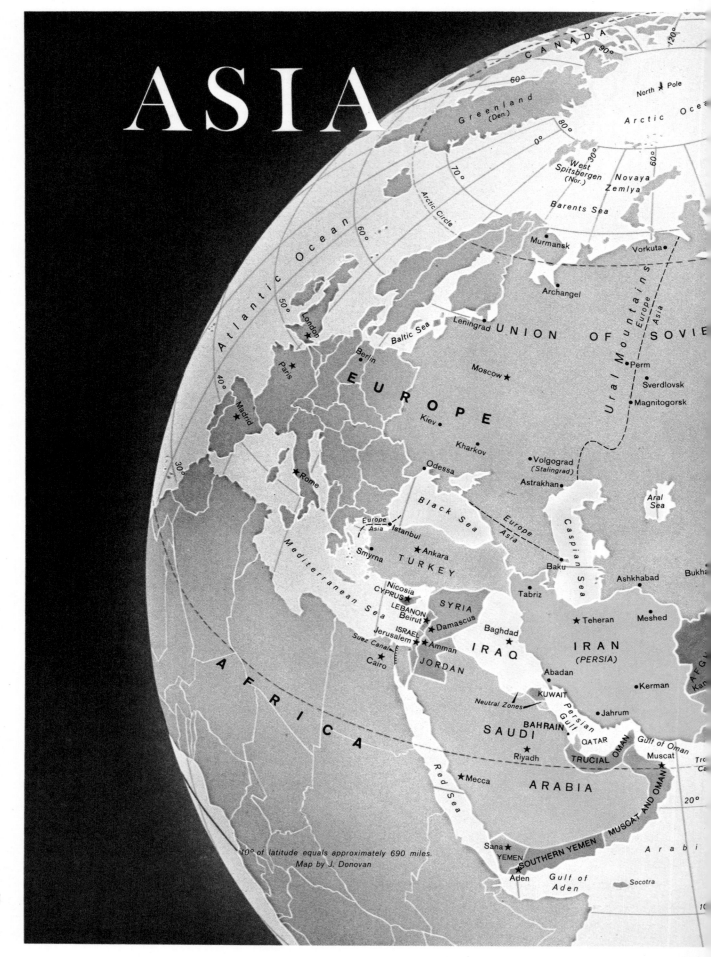

CANADA

North Pole

Arctic Ocean

Greenland (Den.)

West Spitsbergen (Nor.)

Novaya Zemlya

Barents Sea

Murmansk

Vorkuta

Atlantic Ocean

Arctic Circle

Archangel

Ural Mountains

Europe / Asia

London

Baltic Sea

Leningrad

UNION OF SOVIET

Perm

Berlin

Paris

EUROPE

Moscow

Sverdlovsk

Magnitogorsk

Madrid

Kiev

Kharkov

Volgograd (Stalingrad)

Aral Sea

Rome

Odessa

Astrakhan

Black Sea

Europe / Asia

Caspian Sea

Baku

Ashkhabad

Bukha

Europe Asia

Istanbul

Tabriz

Meshed

Mediterranean Sea

Smyrna

Ankara

TURKEY

Teheran

IRAN (PERSIA)

Nicosia

CYPRUS

SYRIA

LEBANON Beirut

Damascus

Baghdad

ISRAEL

Jerusalem

Amman

IRAQ

Suez Canal

Cairo

JORDAN

Abadan

Kerman

AFG Kan

AFRICA

Neutral Zones

KUWAIT

Jahrum

Persian Gulf

BAHRAIN

SAUDI

QATAR

OMAN

Gulf of Oman

Muscat

Tr Ca

Riyadh

TRUCIAL

MUSCAT AND OMAN

Red Sea

Mecca

ARABIA

20°

Sana

SOUTHERN YEMEN

Arabi

10° of latitude equals approximately 690 miles.
Map by J. Donovan

YEMEN

Aden

Gulf of Aden

Socotra

10

38

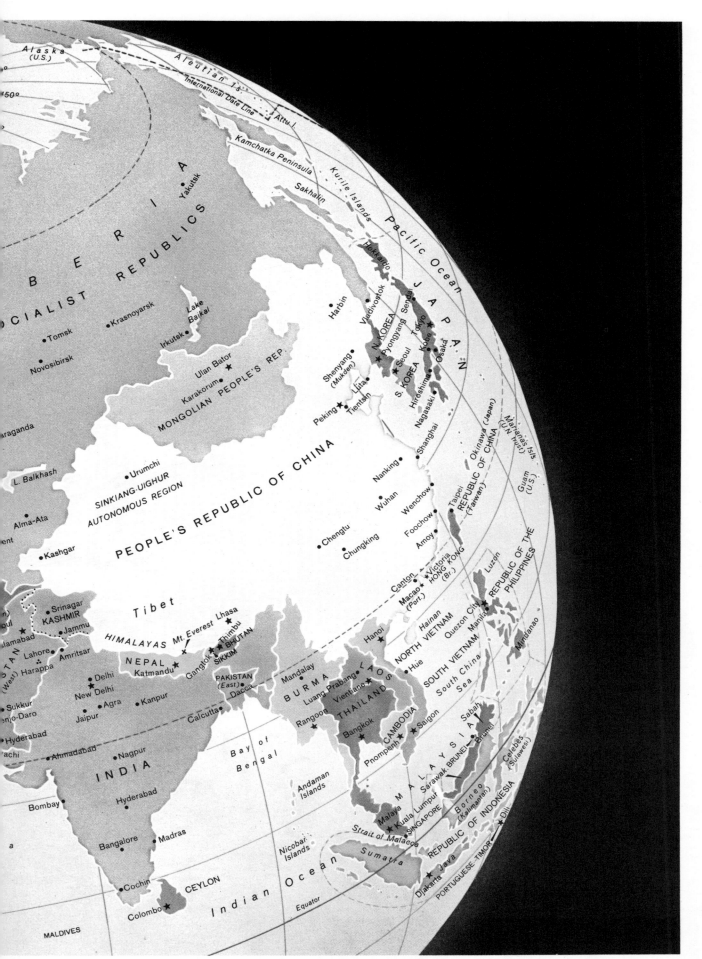

Alaska
(U.S.)

Aleutian Is.

International Date Line

Attu I.

Kamchatka Peninsula

Kurile Islands

Pacific Ocean

S   I   B   E   R   I   A

Yakutsk

Sakhalin

CIALIST   REPUBLICS

OCIALIST

Tomsk   Krasnoyarsk
                                        Irkutsk   Lake
                                                            Baikal
    Novosibirsk

Hokkaido

Harbin

Vladivostok

N. KOREA

J   A   P   A   N

Ulan Bator

Karakorum

MONGOLIAN PEOPLE'S REP.

Pyongyang Sendai
                Tokyo

Shenyang
(Mukden)
                Liuta
Peking Tientsin

Seoul   Kobe
S. KOREA   Osaka

Hiroshima

Nagasaki

Shanghai

raganda

L. Balkhash

Urumchi

SINKIANG-UIGHUR

AUTONOMOUS REGION

PEOPLE'S   REPUBLIC   OF   CHINA

Nanking

Wuhan

Chengtu

Chungking

Wenchow

Foochow

Amy

Republic of China

Okinawa (Japan)

Marianas Isls
(UN trust)

Guam
(U.S.)

Taipei REPUBLIC OF CHINA
        (Taiwan)

Alma-Ata

Kashgar

Tibet

Srinagar
KASHMIR
        Jammu

HIMALAYAS Mt. Everest Lhasa
                        Thimbu
                    Gangtok BHUTAN
NEPAL   SIKKIM
Katmandu

Canton
Macao
(Port.) Victoria
        HONG KONG
        (Br.)

Hainan

Luzon

REPUBLIC OF THE
PHILIPPINES

lamabad

Lahore Amritsar
(West) Harappa

Delhi

New Delhi

Jaipur Agra   Kanpur

PAKISTAN
(East)
Dacca

Mandalay

B U R M A

Luang Prabang

Hanoi

Hüe

NORTH VIETNAM

SOUTH VIETNAM

Quezon City
Manila

South China

Mindanao

enjo-Daro

Hyderabad

achi

Ahmadabad

Nagpur

I N D I A

Bombay

Hyderabad

Bangalore Madras

Calcutta

Rangoon

L A O S

Vientiane

THAILAND

Bangkok

CAMBODIA

Saigon

Pnompenh

Sea

Sabah
Brunei

Sarawak BRUNEI

M A L A Y S I A

Celebes
(Sulawesi)

a

Cochin CEYLON

Colombo

MALDIVES

Bay of
Bengal

Andaman
Islands

Nicobar
Islands

Equator

Malaya Kuala Lumpur
        SINGAPORE
Strait of Malacca

Sumatra

Borneo
(Kalimantan)

REPUBLIC OF INDONESIA

Djakarta Java PORTUGUESE TIMOR Dili

Indian   Ocean

39

miles, it occupies almost 30 percent of the earth's surface. Asia is where the first civilizations began and where the great religions were born. It is also where the languages spoken by most of the people of the world originated."

LIKE A MAGNET

It is interesting to note that ever since ancient times Asia and Europe, which, after all, form a single landmass, have been attracted to each other. This attraction has been like that of opposite poles of a magnet. I must add that the relationship between the two continents has not always been peaceful. Quite the other way. The Europeans may have started the trouble when, according to the legend of the Trojan War, the Greeks crossed into western Asia and besieged and then

destroyed the city of Troy. The Persians returned the favor by invading Europe to attack Greece. Then it was the turn of Europe again, when Alexander the Great led his Macedonian soldiers in a series of conquests. These conquests took them as far east as the Indus River in what is now Pakistan. Later successive waves of Huns, Mongols, and Turks from the heart of Asia overran much of eastern Europe.

Meanwhile Europe was sending explorers, merchants, and missionaries to Asia. They brought back accounts of the wonders of its civilizations and its fabulous riches. One of the first to describe these wonders was Marco Polo, who journeyed from the Italian city of Venice to the court of Kublai Khan in China, passing through much of Asia on the way.

It is an unpleasant fact that for many centuries almost all of Asia was subject to European domination. The vast and wealthy continent was carved up into colonies by the various European countries. Its wealth was exploited for the benefit of these countries. It was not until very recent times that Asia was able to regain the independence it had in its glorious past.

A LAND OF EXTREMES

But now Donald has his encyclopedia out again, and he is about to read to us from it:

"Asia is so enormous," continued our expert, "that it includes all three of the world's climatic zones—the Arctic, temperate, and torrid zones. And since so much of the land is so far from the sea, great extremes in temperature are found.

Left: Women workers in the Indian city of Ahmadabad place hand-dyed and printed rugs and fabrics out in the sun to dry.

41

In fact, Asia has some of the hottest as well as the coldest temperatures on earth."

"Just how hot and how cold?" interrupted the skeptical Panchito.

"Well," replied Donald, as he consulted his references, "in Siberia the lowest temperature outside Antarctica has been recorded—over 90 degrees below zero Fahrenheit. On the other hand, in Israel temperatures of 129 degrees Fahrenheit have been recorded."

"I think I'm freezing," groaned José Carioca.

"That 125-degree heat is making me perspire," added Dumbo.

Donald ignored them and continued to read:

"Asia has both the highest point in the world and the lowest place on the surface of the earth. Mount Everest, which lies on the border between Nepal and Tibet and is part of the great Himalayan range, soars 29,028 feet into the sky. It is the world's highest mountain peak. The Dead Sea, a salt lake in Israel, lies some 1,300 feet below sea level. It is the lowest spot on the face of the globe."

"Well, I'm impressed," admitted Panchito. "Tell us some more about Asia," asked José Carioca and Dumbo together.

Donald picked up his book again and continued:

"Many of the plants that provide man with important foods were first grown in Asia and later imported to Europe and to other parts of the world. These include rice and other grains. Asia produces more rice than the rest of the world. This is not surprising since rice is the staple food of many of the people of Asia. The chief rice-producing countries are China, India,

Opposite page, top: A busy square along the waterfront of Singapore, formerly a British colony. The island country became fully independent in 1965. Opposite page, bottom: Houses with beehive-shaped domes in which some Bedouin tribesmen in Syria live.
Above: Tall buildings made of clay bricks are a feature of Shibam, a city in Yemen (Aden).

Indonesia, Bangladesh, Japan, Thailand, South Korea, South Vietnam, and the Philippines. Wheat is the important food grain in North China, Pakistan, northern India, and in Soviet Asia.

"Some of the other important agricultural products of Asia are sugarcane (from India, Indonesia, and Taiwan); tea (China, Ceylon, India, Indonesia, and Japan); cotton (China, India, and Pakistan); rubber (Malaysia and Indonesia); jute, which is used to make sacks, burlap, and twine (Bangladesh); spices. . . ."

"Spices?" it was Panchito again.　43

Above: A traveling rug merchant stands
near his gaily-decorated van on the outskirts
of Bamian, Afghanistan. The caves seen in
the cliff behind the truck were used by
Buddhist monks centuries ago.
Right: Many Muslim women still veil their
faces. This Afghan woman is covered from
head to toe in a shroudlike garment called
a chaderi.

"Didn't they have something to do with the discovery of America?"

"That's right," added José Carioca. "Christopher Columbus was looking for a shorter route to Asia when he discovered America. And one of the things he was looking for in Asia was spices."

"Wasn't that a long trip to make just for some spices?" asked Dumbo.

"Spices were greatly prized. They made food taste better, and were also used to disguise the taste of spoiled food—for there were no refrigerators in those days," José Carioca reminded him. "Spices were worth their weight in gold!"

"Ahem," muttered Donald, "If I may be allowed to continue.

"One of the most valuable natural resources of Asia is oil. Most of it comes

from a small area of Southwest Asia, especially Saudi Arabia, Iran, Kuwait, Iraq, and the United Arab Emirates. This region produces more oil than any other in the world."

FROM TUNDRA TO TROPICS

"The plant and animal life of Asia is

Above and opposite page: The Mongols have been expert horsemen since the days when their warrior ancestors rode with Genghis Khan and Tamerlane.

46

as varied as the climate. In the far north is a region of tundra, or almost barren plains, covered here and there with mosses and lichens. There are polar bears, seals, and reindeer. To the south we find vast areas of pine forest, swamps and lakes, brown bear, deer, fox, otter, ermine, marten, and sable.

"Further south runs a grassy steppe that borders a region of deserts extending from the Gobi of Mongolia to Saudi Arabia. Here are found hyena, jackal, antelope, gazelle, and the camel. Just to the south lies the high plateau of Tibet, the home of the yak. The yak resembles a kind of shaggy buffalo and serves as a

47

beast of burden and a source of food, clothing, and shelter for the Tibetans.

"Finally we come to tropical Asia, a land of lush vegetation and fertile soil. This is the home of the tiger, leopard, elephant, water buffalo, various kinds of monkeys, snakes (including the giant python and the deadly cobra), and a host of brilliantly colored birds. This region is sometimes called Monsoon Asia, because of the monsoon winds. The summer monsoons bring the heavy rains that make this the great rice-growing area of Asia.

"Asia has enormous mountain ranges that extend for thousands of miles. They include the Himalayas, the Karakoram, and the Hindu Kush. Asia also has great rivers, such as the Yangtze (the longest in Asia) and the Yellow of China; the Ganges, Brahmaputra, and Indus of India and Pakistan; the Mekong and Salween of Southeast Asia; and the Tigris and Euphrates of Southwest Asia. Man's first civilizations were born along these rivers."

As Donald paused to catch his breath, Dumbo asked: "What about the people?"

"Asia has many different peoples," Donald replied. "Eastern Asia is the home of Mongoloid peoples, whose typical representatives include the Mongols, Chinese, and Japanese. Southwest Asia has a mixture of Malays and Mongoloids. The Indo-Aryans, who resemble Europeans, though they may be somewhat darker, live in the Indian subcontinent and Iran. Semitic peoples include the Arabs and Jews of Southwest Asia. Turkic groups are found in Central Asia and Turkey. The Ainu of northern Japan and the Negritos of southern Asia are two small but distinct racial groups."

CHINA

"That's enough general information, I think," said Donald. "Now let's visit some of the important nations of Asia. We'll start with China."

"Why China?" asked the argumentative Panchito.

"Because China's 3,700,000 square miles make it the largest country in Asia and the third largest in the world," explained Donald. "It is also the most heavily populated nation on earth. It has approximately 750,000,000 people, rep-

48

Above: Rice is the most important crop grown in the Philippines, where about 65 percent of the people are farmers. The Philippines consists of some 7,000 islands. The largest islands are Luzon in the north and Mindanao in the south. Right: Muslims in Kashmir bow in prayer during a religious ceremony. Kashmir, which is located in the Himalaya mountains, is presently divided between Pakistan and India.

resenting almost one quarter of all mankind.

"This immense country can be divided into two very different parts—eastern and western. Eastern China is where most of the people live. It has most of the good land, including the fertile valleys of the Yangtze and Yellow rivers. This is the heart of the country's agriculture. The northeastern region, sometimes known as Manchuria, is a center of China's heavy industry. Western China is made up partly of mountainous regions and partly of desert and steppe. In the southwest lies Tibet, which is now under the control of China. Western China is more suitable to the raising of livestock than to agriculture.

"China has a recorded history thousands of years old. It was one of the most highly developed of all the world's great civilizations. Paper, printing, and gunpowder were just a few of the inventions that originated in China. China ruled as

Above: a fishing village on the island of Hong Kong, a British colony off the southeastern coast of China.

Opposite page: A Southeast Asian river town during the height of the monsoon rains. The monsoon is a seasonal wind that blows across Southeast Asia in the summer. It is accompanied by heavy rains, which often result in disastrous flooding.

50

a great power in Asia for centuries, until, during the 19th century, it came into contact with the West.

"China was no match for the highly industrialized nations of Europe, and it was forced to submit to trade and other conditions imposed by these nations. In 1911 the last of the imperial dynasties, or ruling families, was overthrown, and China became a republic under Sun Yat-sen. After World War II civil war raged between the Communists under Mao Tse-tung and the Nationalists under Chiang Kai-shek. The Communists were victorious and in 1949 established the People's Republic of China ruled from the ancient capital of Peking. The nationalists maintained themselves on the island of Taiwan.

"China is still dependent on agriculture to feed its many millions of people. But in recent years it has made remarkable strides in industry and is on its way to becoming a great industrial power."

Donald stopped to catch his breath again and sighed. "There are so many things to say about China. But we must stop here and go on to our next destination."

JAPAN

"See those four large islands down there? They are called Hokkaido, Honshu, Kyushu, and Chikoku. Together with many smaller islands they make up Japan. It is not a large country. It is a little less than 146,000 square miles in area, or smaller than California. But it has a population of over 104,000,000. Japan is mostly a mountainous land with many volcanoes, the most famous being the beautiful Mount Fuji.

"Since so much of Japan is mountainous, the fertile land is cultivated carefully, and a large percentage of the population is engaged in agriculture. Fishing is very important and Japan ranks second in the world in this industry, just behind Peru. Japan is among the three or four most highly industrialized nations in the world. Only the United States and the Soviet Union rank ahead of Japan. It is the foremost shipbuilding country, one of the leading iron and steel producers, and is second in the manufacture of automobiles. Tokyo, Japan's capital, is the world's largest city, with over 11,000,000 people.

"Although strongly influenced by China, Japan over the centuries developed its own distinct culture. For many years the country lived in isolation, ruled by its emperors and shoguns, or military leaders. Then, in the middle of the 19th century, an American naval officer, Commodore Matthew Perry, arrived in Japan with several warships, and Japan was opened to the world. It developed quickly into a modern nation and a military power. Much of Japan was destroyed during World War II, but in the years since, Japan has re-established itself as one of the world's leading nations."

Unfortunately, we must end our too short visit to Japan. Taking a cherry tree blossom with them as a souvenir, our travelers boarded Dumbo again. They flew west, crossing Korea, itself a land of ancient culture, China again, and Mongolia. Donald reminded the others that in the 13th century Genghis Khan and his Mongol horsemen had conquered

A giant reclining Buddha looks out at worshipers in a pagoda (Buddhist temple) at Pegu. The city of Pegu was the capital of Burma in the 16th century, during the Toungoo dynasty. Nearly all of the people of Burma are Buddhists, and the religion plays an important part in their daily lives.

53

Above: The Dome of the Rock, a Muslim shrine in Jerusalem. It is on the site of the ancient First Temple of Israel.

much of Asia. But the Mongols have been peaceful for centuries. Then the travelers soared due south. They crossed the vastness of central China to a region that has been very much in the news in recent years.

SOUTHEAST ASIA

Alighting, Donald thumbed through his encyclopedia to the correct entry:

"The countries that make up Southeast Asia," he read, "are Burma, Thailand, Laos, North and South Vietnam, Cambodia, Malaysia, Singapore, Indonesia, and the Philippines, Laos, Cambodia, and Vietnam are sometimes referred to as Indochina. The largest of the Southeast Asian countries and the richest in natural resources is Indonesia. The fabled Spice Islands, which drew European explorers, were in Indonesia. The smallest of the countries of Southeast Asia is the island nation of Singapore.

"The region may be divided into two parts: mainland Southeast Asia and the

archipelagoes, or groups of islands, such as Indonesia and the Philippines. It covers an area of over 1,738,000 square miles and is inhabited by approximately 280,-000,000 people. It lies in the heart of the monsoon belt and the seasons are alternately wet and dry. Rice is the chief agricultural product. Mineral resources are still largely undeveloped. Most of the people are Buddhists and magnificent temples can be found through much of the region."

THE INDIAN SUBCONTINENT

From Southeast Asia to the Indian subcontinent was only a short flight westward. Upon landing, Donald immediately resumed his lecture:

"In 1947 Great Britain granted independence to its Indian empire, which it had ruled for 3 centuries. Because of religious and other differences among the people, the land was divided into two separate nations: India, whose people are mainly Hindu, and Pakistan, a largely Muslim country. Just recently Pakistan itself underwent a bloody civil war and its eastern part declared its independence as Bangladesh. Bangladesh is the world's newest nation.

"India is by far the largest country in this region (which is also called South Asia) and one of the largest in the world. It has over 1,260,000 square miles and more than 530,000,000 people. It is second only to China in population.

"Some 4,000 years ago a great civilization developed in the valley of the Indus River in what is now Pakistan. About 1500 B.C. a people from the north destroyed this civilization and gradually spread over most of the subcontinent. These people are usually called Indo-

Aryans. They spoke a language that was to be the mother tongue of many European and Indian languages spoken today. They also brought their own customs and culture, which eventually became the religion of Hinduism. They are the ancestors of the present inhabitants of Pakistan and northern India.

"Many other peoples entered India over the centuries. All left their mark on the land and its people. Monuments of these various cultures can still be seen across the landscape. Ancient and new India mix in the great cities. There are Calcutta and Bombay, with their populations of 5,000,000 and more; Madras, with 2,000,000 people, the chief city of southern India; and New Delhi, the modern capital of the country.

"Since independence India has had many obstacles to overcome. Growing enough food to feed its people, improving the standards of education, and trying to industrialize the country are just a few of the tasks India faces.

"Along the rim of the subcontinent to the north lie Afghanistan, a mountainous land that borders Pakistan, and the Himalayan kingdoms of Nepal, Sikkim, and Bhutan. Also in the north is the princely state of Kashmir, which both India and Pakistan claim. To the south lies the lovely pearl-shaped island of Ceylon, and to the southeast the island chain called the Maldives."

Donald paused again and this time he took a very deep breath. "We have one more stop to make in Asia. We are going to a region that geographers call Southwest Asia. Some people refer to it as part of the Middle East."

SOUTHWEST ASIA

The hop to Southwest Asia was soon completed and Donald settled himself comfortably before continuing:

"The countries of Southwest Asia are Turkey, Cyprus, Syria, Lebanon, Israel, Jordan, Saudi Arabia, the two Yemens, Kuwait, the small states of Oman, Bahrain, Qatar, and the United Arab Emirates, Iraq, and Iran.

"Turkey has the distinction of being both in Asia and Europe, although only a tiny part of the country lies in Europe. The inhabitants of the island of Cyprus are of Greek and Turkish descent. Modern Turkey is only a fraction of the once vast empire of the Ottoman Turks. Iran, formerly called Persia, recalls the once great Persian Empire. Except for the Greeks on Cyprus and the Jews of Israel, most of the people of this region are Muslims, followers of the religion called Islam. The founder of the faith was the 8th-century prophet Mohammed, and the Arabian Peninsula was its birthplace. Judaism, the faith of the Jews, and Christianity were born in what is now Israel. A new nation in an old land, Israel came into existence in 1949. It was founded by Jews, who had suffered persecution for centuries and wished to reclaim their ancient homeland. In Iraq and Syria, along the Tigris and Euphrates rivers, the ancient cities of Sumer and Babylon once flourished and influenced the growth of Western civilization.

"The greatest natural resource of Southwest Asia is oil, without which modern life could not continue. Some of the smallest countries in the world are among the richest in oil. They are the tiny sheikhdoms and emirates that lie along the Persian Gulf."

"That concludes our visit to Asia," said Donald. "Now let's get ready for a jump across the Ural Mountains to Europe."

A YOUNG LADY NAMED EUROPA

Now Donald told his friends the old Greek legend about the king of the gods and the beautiful princess. "Once upon a time there was a young princess named Europa. Because of her beauty, the god Zeus fell in love with her. He transformed himself into a white bull and offered Europa a ride across the sea on his back. Europa happily accepted his exciting offer, and soon she was crossing the waters to Crete on Zeus's back."

"And that's how the continent of Europe got its name?" asked José Carioca.

"Maybe," answered Donald. "Some people say it is. But there are others who believe that the name was invented by the people of the ancient Middle East. They called the lands east of them *Asu*— "land of the rising sun"—from which we get the name Asia. They called the lands west of them *Ereb*—"land of the setting sun"—or Europe.

"If a continent is defined as a large landmass surrounded by water, why do we call Europe a continent?" Panchito asked.

Donald, who had studied hard for his travels, answered Panchito easily.

"Good question, Panchito," Donald replied. "There is still a big debate about whether Europe should be called a continent. On a map Europe looks like—and in fact is—a peninsula jutting westward off the Asian landmass. Some geographers think of Europe and Asia as one continent, which they call Eurasia. But most geographers still think of Europe as a separate continent for two reasons. One is that Europe has played a highly distinctive and important role in history. The other reason is that Europe can be seen as a continent with well-marked borders.

In the north, west, and south these borders are the seas. In the east the border is usually drawn through the Ural Mountains and south to the Caspian Sea.

"Because this line goes right through the Soviet Union," Donald said, "that country is unevenly divided between Europe and Asia. Many geographers place all of the U.S.S.R. within Europe because its history has been European and some of its leading industries and its major cities, such as the capital, Moscow, are in Europe.

"Oh, boy," Panchito sighed, "it's complicated. And the U.S.S.R. looks so big, and Europe looks so little."

"You're right," said Donald. "The continent of Europe with the slice of the U.S.S.R. included, plus some nearby islands, covers only about 4,200,000 square miles. The only continent smaller is Australia. Yet the entire Soviet Union covers over twice the area of Europe— or about 8,650,000 square miles.

Opposite page: The Thames River flows by the Houses of Parliament in London, capital of the United Kingdom. Below: Windmill at Leimuiden in the Netherlands. These two pictures capture something of the variety and fascination of Europe, one of mankind's oldest centers of civilization.

"Hey," Donald exclaimed, "I have a great idea. Let's start our tour of Europe with the Soviet Union because it is the biggest country in Europe."

The words were no sooner out of his mouth than Dumbo was airborne, carrying our travelers over the varied landscape of the Soviet Union—home of 241,000,000 people.

THE U.S.S.R.—A GIANT NATION

"The Soviet Union, or Union of Soviet Socialist Republics, as it is officially called," said Donald, "stretches from the Baltic Sea to the Pacific Ocean and from the Arctic Ocean to the borders of Turkey, Iran, and Afghanistan. You won't be a bit surprised, I'll bet, to learn that it is the world's largest nation.

"Considering its size," Donald went on, "you won't be surprised either to find that the U.S.S.R. has nearly every kind of landscape and climate. You can freeze in the northern regions of the Soviet Union in the winter and bake in the dry, hot climate along the southern borders. In the areas in between you will find many variations of temperature, but on

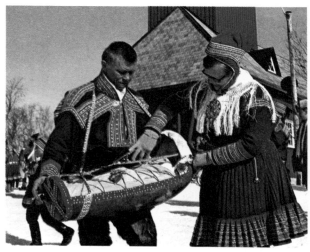

Norwegian Lapps wearing their typical brightly-colored costumes. Opposite page: One of Norway's many magnificent fjords, as these deep inlets of the sea are called.

58

the whole, winters are generally long and summers short and not too hot.

"The Soviet Union can boast of some of the most remarkable natural wonders in Europe. They include the highest mountain, Elbrus in the Caucasus, and the longest river, the Volga. The Volga is as important to the U.S.S.R. as the Mississippi is to the United States.

"In addition the Soviet Union has a wealth of the metals and other minerals needed for modern industry. It is one of the world's leading producers of coal, iron, petroleum, copper, nickel, bauxite (the ore of aluminum), and such precious meals as gold, silver, and platinum.

"Agriculture is of great importance to this vast nation, too. The products of Soviet collective farms include large amounts of wheat, rye, corn, oats, and sugar beets. Fruit is raised in the warm southern regions and in parts of the east.

"The people of the Soviet Union are as varied as its landscape and products. The major language, Russian, is spoken by a little more than half the population. Such traditional languages as Ukrainian, Belorussian, Lithuanian, Latvian, Estonian, Moldavian, Yiddish, Uzbek, and Tatar are also heard. As a result, on a walk along the streets in one of the major cities you might hear any one of a dozen or more languages. You might see people who look like Europeans, Asians, Arabs, or almost any other nationality you can think of. They might be dressed as shepherds or nomads, or perhaps in ordinary business suits. We could spend months enjoying the variety and color of the U.S.S.R., but we must move on to visit the U.S.S.R.'s neighbors in the west. We'll start with the seven nations of Eastern Europe, which are closely related to the Soviet Union historically and politically.

Opposite page: The Grossglockner, Austria's highest peak. Above: A marble quarry in Italy's Apuane Alps, an important source of fine marble.

61

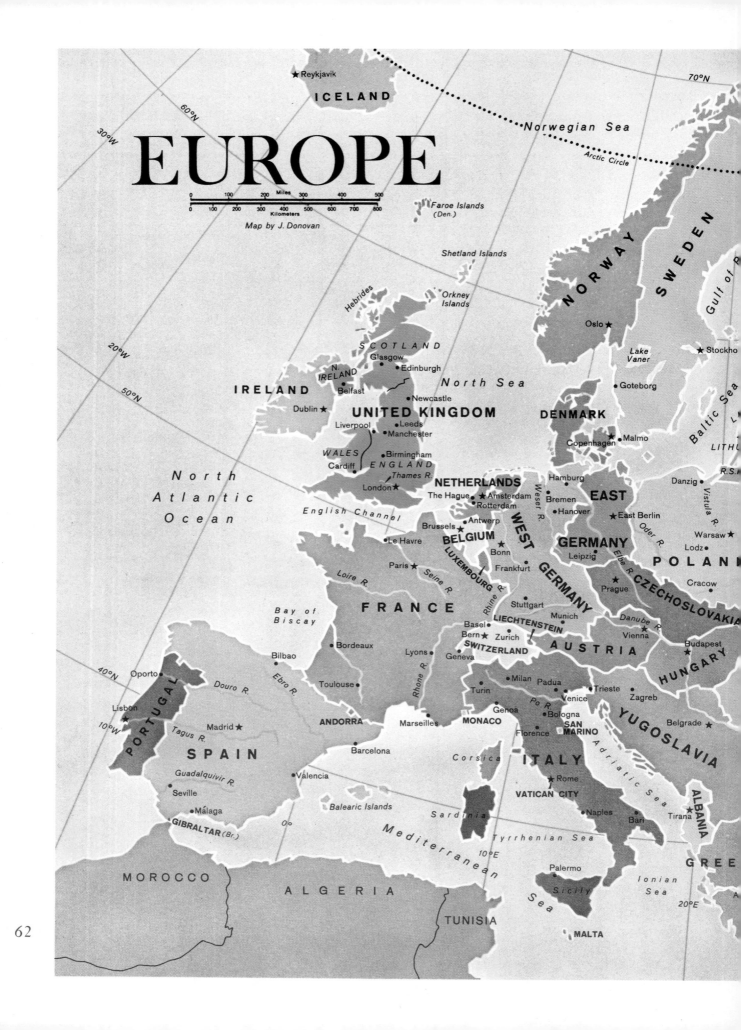

EUROPE

Map by J. Donovan

Barents
Sea

Murmansk

White
Sea

Archangel

FINLAND

Lake
Onega

Lake
Ladoga

sinki

Leningrad

ESTONIA

nn

RUSSIAN SOVIET FEDERATED SOCIALIST REPUBLIC

Volga R.

Gorki

Kazan

Ufa

★ Moscow

Kuibyshev

UNION OF SOVIET SOCIALIST REPUBLICS

Minsk

BELORUSSIA

Saratov

KAZAKHSTAN

Kursk

Aral
Sea

Kiev

Kharkov

UZBEKISTAN

Poltava

UKRAINE

Volgograd
(Stalingrad)

Dnepropetrovsk

Don R.

Dniester R.

Krivoi Rog

Donetsk
(Stalino)

Rostov

MOLDAVIA

RUMANIA

Kishinev

Odessa

Sea of
Azov

Caspian Sea

TURKMENIA

Yalta

Europe
Asia

Caucasus

Bucharest

GEORGIA

Baku

Constanta

Black Sea

40°E

AZERBAIJAN

anube R.

LGARIA

ARMENIA

50°E

vdiv

Bosporus

Istanbul

Europe
Asia

★ Ankara

Teheran

Dardanelles

TURKEY

IRAN

se

SYRIA

IRAQ

CYPRUS

30°E

Baghdad
★

te

GLOBE INSET:

North Pole

NORTH AMERICA

GREENLAND

Arctic
Ocean

Novaya
Zemlya

ASIA

Atlantic
Ocean

EUROPE

AFRICA

Equator

EAST EUROPE

"The nations of East Europe—Poland, Czechoslovakia, Hungary, Bulgaria, Rumania, Albania, and Yugoslavia—are often grouped together," said Donald, "because they occupy a long strip of land on the historic route leading from north to south and east to west in Europe.

"The peoples of Poland, Czechoslovakia, Bulgaria, and Yugoslavia are mainly Slavs, the most numerous people in Europe. They speak Slavic languages related to Russian. The Albanians speak an ancient tongue. The Hungarians of today are descended from the Magyars and speak a language that is distantly related to Finnish and Estonian. The Rumanians proudly claim descent from the Romans who settled in their country centuries ago. And they speak a language that is quite closely related to such Romance languages as Italian, French, and Spanish.

"You can see from the map," Donald said, "that these nations stretch from north to south across central Europe. You've probably guessed, then, that the climate depends on where you are—whether it's north in Poland along the Baltic coast or on Yugoslavia's beautiful, sunny Adriatic coast. The landscape varies from the plains, or *pole*, that gave Poland its name to the mountains that cut across Czechoslovakia, Rumania, Bulgaria, Yugoslavia, and Albania. And you can understand from their positions on the coast why Poland, Yugoslavia, and Albania are seafaring nations. The mighty Danube River provides Czechoslovakia, Hungary, Bulgaria, and Rumania with an important inland water route that ends in a beautiful bird-filled delta on the Black Sea.

"Until recently all these nations, except Czechoslovakia and Poland, were mainly farming nations. Agriculture is still important, but industries are growing rapidly all over East Europe.

"No visit to East Europe is complete without at least a quick tour of its capital cities—Warsaw on the Vistula River in Poland; Prague on the banks of the Moldau in Czechoslovakia; and, perhaps most beautiful of all, Budapest on the Danube in Hungary. Sofia, Bulgaria's capital, is known for its roses, and Bucharest, the capital of Rumania, for its broad boulevards. And we must not forget Belgrade, Yugosalvia's modern capital city. Tirana, Albania's capital, is an exotic mixture of old and new, Turkish and European.

SOUTHERN EUROPE

"Since we have traveled so far south," suggested Donald, "Why don't we hop from one southern European peninsula to another?" His friends thought that this was a good idea, and before long they were circling on Dumbo's back over Greece, the cradle of European civilization. Before they started touring, Donald explained that all three of the peninsulas that jut out of Europe into the Mediterranean Sea had probably been settled since before men began keeping historical records. He went on to say that since the earliest days these ancient lands had been important seafaring nations. Like Scandinavia and Britain in the north, they had had a powerful impact on the history of the Western world.

Then, looking down, Donald shouted excitedly, "Look! There is Zeus's home on Mount Olympus and there is the site of the world's first Olympic Games. And there—there is Athens, the greatest city of the ancient world." Our travelers could not believe their eyes, for there below them, spread out on a hill above the

Above: a crop of grain is harvested in southern Portugal, which is known for its long growing season.

modern capital, were the ruins of the old city. They gazed at old Athens, home of the philosophers and statesmen who laid the foundations for Western ideas that are still important today.

Now our excited travelers headed for another great center of the ancient world —the Italian peninsula. On this crowded peninsula today there are three countries —the Republic of Italy, Vatican City, and the very small state of San Marino, which is tucked off in a corner.

Italy is the largest nation on the Italian peninsula. Bounded by the Alps on the north and with the Apennines running as a backbone along its entire length, Italy is a land with few large farming areas. Today the products of industry plus tourism provide much of its income. Its capital, Rome, is a treasure-house of

Above: A dike on the Zuider Zee in the Netherlands —one of the means by which the Dutch defend their low-lying land from the sea. Below: Rotterdam, a major port of the Netherlands and of Europe.

Above: On November 14, 1963, a spectacular volcanic eruption took place in the sea off Iceland. It marked the birth of a new island, which has been given the name of Surtsey.
Below: The gentle Liffey River flows through Dublin, the capital and leading city of Eire, as the independent Republic of Ireland is sometimes called.

68

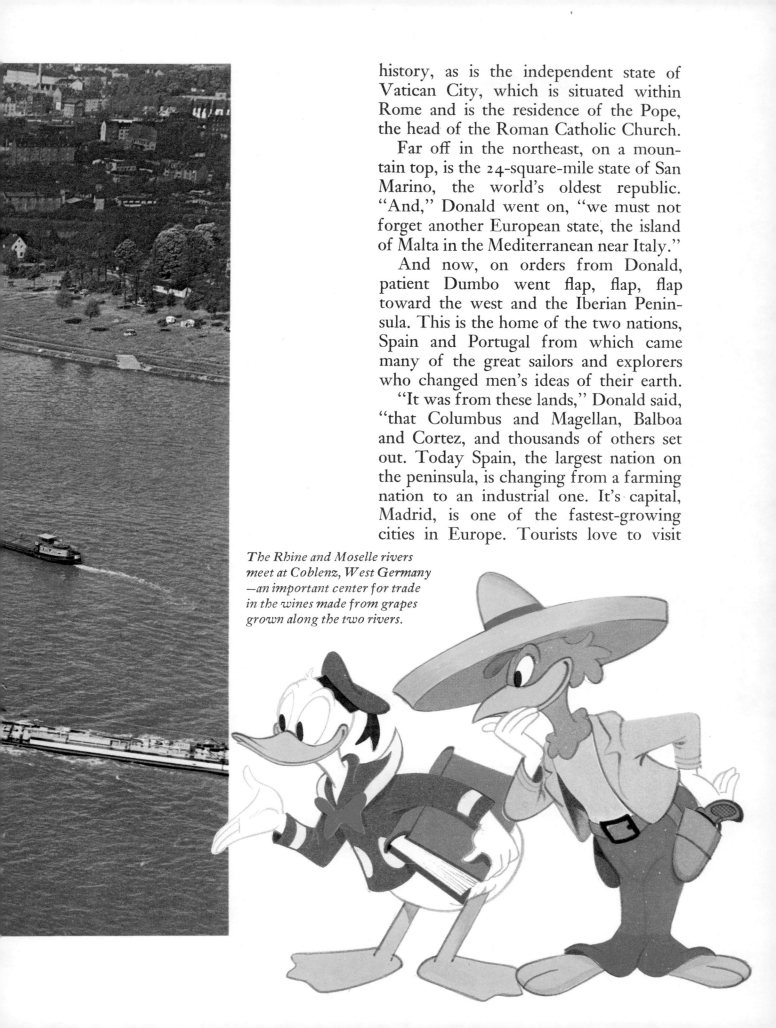

history, as is the independent state of Vatican City, which is situated within Rome and is the residence of the Pope, the head of the Roman Catholic Church.

Far off in the northeast, on a mountain top, is the 24-square-mile state of San Marino, the world's oldest republic. "And," Donald went on, "we must not forget another European state, the island of Malta in the Mediterranean near Italy."

And now, on orders from Donald, patient Dumbo went flap, flap, flap toward the west and the Iberian Peninsula. This is the home of the two nations, Spain and Portugal from which came many of the great sailors and explorers who changed men's ideas of their earth.

"It was from these lands," Donald said, "that Columbus and Magellan, Balboa and Cortez, and thousands of others set out. Today Spain, the largest nation on the peninsula, is changing from a farming nation to an industrial one. It's capital, Madrid, is one of the fastest-growing cities in Europe. Tourists love to visit

The Rhine and Moselle rivers meet at Coblenz, West Germany —an important center for trade in the wines made from grapes grown along the two rivers.

Spain. They enjoy its historic landmarks and fine beaches. Portugal, too, off in the west, is slowly changing from an agricultural nation to an industrial one. But here, too, it is the monuments of the past and a necklace of lovely beaches that visitors seek."

THE SCANDINAVIAN PENINSULA

Donald whispered to Dumbo and turned to his friends. "For a change of pace," he said, "we are going to fly north

A coal mine in the Rhondda Valley of Wales, a part of the United Kingdom. Opposite page: Workers picking grapes in Burgundy, France.

to Scandinavia, the peninsula and islands on which we will find Denmark, Sweden, Norway, and Finland. These northern countries were also the home of great sailors—the Vikings—and today are among the most advanced industrial nations in the world. Farthest north is Finland with its thousands of lakes and magnificent forests, a source of lumber for industry. Helsinki, the capital, is a lively modern city that is well-known for its architecture. Moving southwest we come to Sweden—a land of lakes, forests, iron mines, and bustling industries. The capital, Stockholm, lies on islands between a lake and the Baltic Sea. Stretched out along the western edge of Scandinavia is Norway. It is still a nation of seafarers, fishermen, and farmers, who make their home along the slopes of mountains that dip down to the sea. The people of Denmark in the south have transformed their country into a major food exporter and industrial leader. Copenhagen, the capital of Denmark, is the site of the world-famous Tivoli Gardens, an amusement park. Iceland, the island in the North Atlantic, was once a part of Denmark but is now an independent republic—a distant but fascinating part of Europe.

WESTERN EUROPE

"Among the most important islands off Europe are the British Isles, seat of the United Kingdom. The United Kingdom is made up of England, Wales, Scotland, and Northern Ireland," explained Donald. "These densely populated islands were the birthplace of the Industrial Revolution and are today still leaders in industry. As the center of the former British Empire, England gave its language, its democratic ideals, and its culture to people in every corner of the world. The capital, London, is still one of the most international of cities and ranks as the world's fourth largest after Tokyo, Shanghai, and New York.

"Also in the British Isles is the Republic of Ireland. Long a part of the United Kingdom, it regained its independence in the 20th century.

"Moving to the mainland of western Europe we find the three small kingdoms of Belgium, the Netherlands, and Luxembourg. All of them have important industries based on nearby coal and iron deposits. These three small but highly advanced nations are neighbors to France and Germany, two of the largest and most important nations on the continent. France is a major farming and industrial nation. But its worldwide fame comes from its beautiful landscapes and its fabulous cities, of which the capital, Paris, is the best-known. Today Germany is divided into two parts—the Federal Republic of Germany, or West Germany, and the German Democratic Republic, or East Germany. Both are industrial giants. They also offer visitors mountains, rivers like the mighty Rhine, and dense forests

A gigantic hangar in an airplane factory at Fulton, Gloucestershire, England. The British have long been leaders in airplane design and building.

72

to balance the sight of so many bustling factories.

"Among the smaller nations of western Europe is Austria. Vienna is the home of the waltz. Liechtenstein, a tiny state, is nestled between Austria and Switzerland. Switzerland is known for such precision products as watches, and for its soaring Alps. But," added Donald, "speaking of Alps, you should remember that they don't belong just to the Swiss. The Alps stretch in a curve across Europe from France to Yugoslavia. They reach their highest point in Mont Blanc on the French-Italian border.

"And now," Donald went on, "one last stop in Europe at the small principality of Monaco with its lovely Mediterranean beaches and tropical gardens. Then we'll ask Dumbo to take us south across the sea to the dramatic lands of Africa."

THIS IS AFRICA

It was hot. The sun burned violently in the cloudless sky. All about them were vast stretches of sand. The heat rose in waves and in the distance the horizon shimmered. Our heroes had landed smack in the middle of the endless Sahara. Fortunately for them there was a pleasant oasis with sparkling water and lovely palm trees nearby. They hurried to it and had their supper on the veranda of one of the small buildings that stood in the center of the oasis. After that they sat about in the cool of the evening talking.

"So this is Africa," Panchito said.

"Yes," said Donald nodding his head like the scholar that he was. "This is Africa."

Panchito gazed at the huge area of sand that lay all around them.

"Is this what we came to," he croaked. "A land of sand? Nothing but sand?"

"It's sand and it's jungle," said José Carioca.

"Jungle?"

"Africa is a continent of nothing but sand and jungle," José Carioca said wisely.

Panchito was about to speak but Donald had already opened his trusty encyclopedia and motioned for silence.

"Here. I shall tell you all about Africa. So listen closely. First it is not all sand. And it is by no means all jungle."

"Then what is it?" interrupted Panchito.

Donald gazed severely at him. "Will you be patient? Africa is a continent that is just tremendous. In fact, it is the second largest continent in the entire world."

"Asia is larger," said José.

"Right. But only Asia. Think of it this way. Africa is so huge that the landmasses of the United States, Europe, India and Japan could fit into it. And there would still be plenty of space left. Now this tremendous continent has a lot of things in it. The largest desert in the

Opposite page: A Tuareg rider astride a camel. The Tuaregs are nomads of the central Sahara.
Below: A Zulu pulling a ricksha on a city street in South Africa.

whole world—the Sahara. We're in it now. Africa has jungles, savannahs (grasslands), and snowcapped mountains.

"In Africa?" asked Panchito with much astonishment. "Snow in Africa? I don't believe it."

"Well, you'd better believe it. Because Mount Kilimanjaro, which is in Tanzania, has snow on its top all year round. It towers to a height of . . . let me see . . . yes, 19,565 feet. Kilimanjaro is the highest point on the entire continent. Now think of this, Panchito. Kilimanjaro with its snowy head high above the clouds is but a short distance from the equator. And you know how hot it can be at the equator!

So you see Africa is a land of many contrasts. It is very hot, it is very cold, it is very dry, it is very rainy. It has clusters of little round huts with mud walls and thatched roofs. It has block after block of modern apartment houses

Opposite page: Typical Tunisian dwellings found in the countryside and on the outskirts of large cities. The thick adobe walls, flat roofs, and tiny windows tell of the hot, dry climate. Above: Citrus fruit is harvested in the Transvaal, South Africa. Below: A view of Isfahan, one of the oldest cities of Iran.

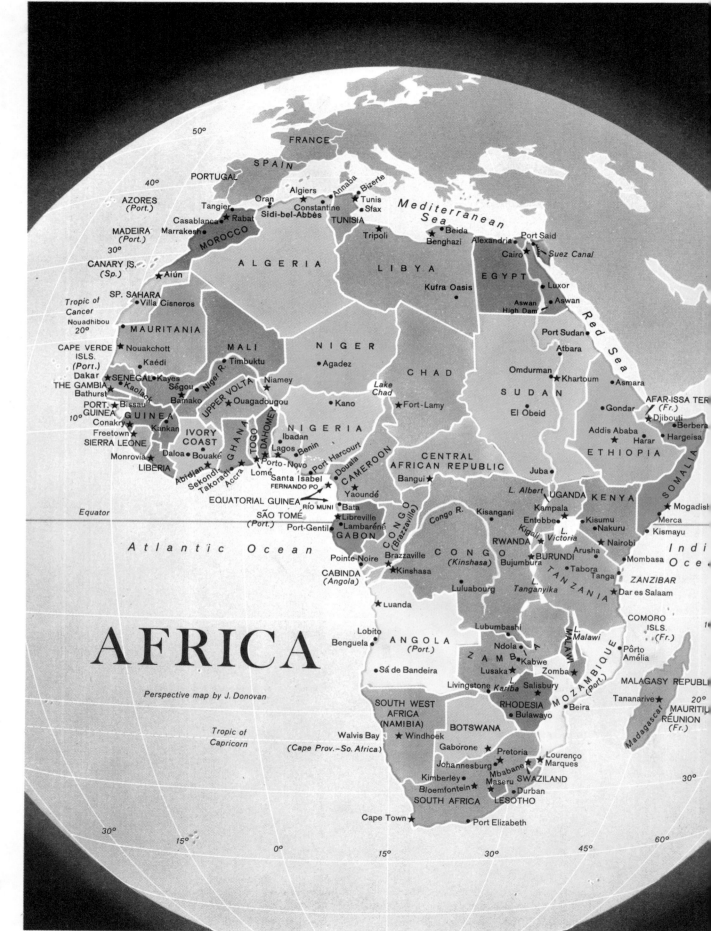

AFRICA

Perspective map by J. Donovan

Mediterranean Sea

Atlantic Ocean

Red Sea

Indian Ocean

FRANCE
SPAIN
PORTUGAL

AZORES
(Port.)

MADEIRA
(Port.)

CANARY IS.
(Sp.)

Tangier
Oran
Algiers
Annaba
Bizerte
Casablanca
Rabat
Constantine
Tunis
Sfax
Sidi-bel-Abbès
Marrakesh
MOROCCO
TUNISIA
Tripoli

Tropic of Cancer

SP. SAHARA
Aíun
ALGERIA
LIBYA
EGYPT
Beida
Benghazi
Alexandria
Port Said
Cairo
Suez Canal
Kufra Oasis
Luxor
Aswan
Aswan High Dam

Nouadhibou
Villa Cisneros
MAURITANIA
MALI
NIGER
CHAD
Port Sudan
Atbara

CAPE VERDE
ISLS.
(Port.)

Nouakchott
Kaédi
Timbuktu
Niger R.
Agadez
Lake Chad
Omdurman
Khartoum
Asmara

Dakar
SENEGAL
Kayes
Ségou
Niamey
Kano
Fort-Lamy
SUDAN
El Obeid
Gondar
AFAR-ISSA TER.
(Fr.)
Djibouti
Berbera
Hargeisa

THE GAMBIA
Bathurst
Kaolack
Bamako
UPPER VOLTA
Ouagadougou
PORT.
GUINEA
Bissau
GUINEA
Conakry
Kankan
IVORY
COAST
GHANA
TOGO
DAHOMEY
NIGERIA
Ibadan
Benin
Lagos
Port Harcourt
CENTRAL
AFRICAN REPUBLIC
Juba
Addis Ababa
Harar
ETHIOPIA
SOMALIA
Mogadishu

Freetown
SIERRA LEONE
Monrovia
LIBERIA
Daloa
Bouaké
Abidjan
Sekondi-
Takoradi
Accra
Lomé
Porto-Novo
Santa Isabel
FERNANDO PO
Douala
Yaoundé
Bangui
L. Albert
UGANDA
Kampala
Entebbe
KENYA
Kisumu
Nakuru
Nairobi
Merca
Kismayu

Equator

EQUATORIAL GUINEA
RÍO MUNI
Bata
CAMEROON
SÃO TOMÉ
(Port.)
Libreville
Lambaréné
Port-Gentil
GABON
CONGO
Kisangani
Congo R.
RWANDA
Kigali
L. Victoria
BURUNDI
Bujumbura
Arusha
Tabora
Mombasa
ZANZIBAR
Indian Ocean

Pointe-Noire
CABINDA
(Angola)
Brazzaville
CONGO
(Kinshasa)
Kinshasa
Luluabourg
TANZANIA
L. Tanganyika
Tanga
Dar es Salaam

Luanda
Lubumbashi
COMORO
ISLS.
(Fr.)
Pôrto
Amélia

ANGOLA
(Port.)
Lobito
Benguela
Ndola
ZAMBIA
Kabwe
MALAWI
L. Malawi
MOZAMBIQUE
(Port.)

Sá de Bandeira
Lusaka
Livingstone
Kariba
Salisbury
Zomba
MALAGASY REPUBLIC
Tananarive

SOUTH WEST
AFRICA
(NAMIBIA)
RHODESIA
Beira
Bulawayo
MAURITIUS
RÉUNION
(Fr.)
Madagascar

Tropic of Capricorn

Walvis Bay
(Cape Prov.–So. Africa)
Windhoek
BOTSWANA
Gaborone
Pretoria
Lourenço Marques
SWAZILAND
Mbabane
Johannesburg
Kimberley
Maseru
LESOTHO
Durban
Bloemfontein
SOUTH AFRICA
Cape Town
Port Elizabeth

50°
40°
30°
20°
10°
0°
15°
30°
45°
60°

78

and quite tall skyscrapers. Africa is the second largest continent and yet it has a fairly small population.

"How large a population does it have?" José asked.

"Well, the latest estimate puts the figure at about 350,000,000."

"That's an awful lot of people," said Panchito.

Donald shook his head.

"Not when you think of a land area of 11,703,861 square miles."

"Are there any large cities in Africa?" Dumbo asked.

"Large cities? Cairo, the capital of Egypt, has a population of over 4,000,000. Way down at the tip of the continent is Johannesburg. This South African city has a population of about 1,150,000. There are other large cities, such as Lagos in Nigeria and Casablanca in Morocco.

And now that we see so many miles of sand all about us, let us think of water. For Africa is a continent of many large rivers and lakes.

THE WATERS

Central Africa is a land of heavy rainfall and high plateaus. And it is here that Africa's great rivers begin. The Nile is one of the longest rivers in the world. Many geographers claim that it is the longest. One of its two main branches, the White Nile, rises in Lake Victoria in east-central Africa. The other, the Blue Nile, begins in Lake Tana in Ethiopia. The Congo is Africa's second longest river. The Niger, third largest of the continent, is the largest river in West Africa. Southern Africa has two major rivers, the Orange and Zambezi. The world-

The mighty Nile, the only African river that crosses the desert without being absorbed by it.

famous Victoria Falls are on the Zambezi River, on the border of Rhodesia and Zambia. This huge waterfall rises to a height of more than 350 feet—that is twice as high as Niagara Falls between the United States and Canada.

Africa has many large lakes. Among them are lakes Edward, Albert, Malawi, Chad, and Tanganyika. Lake Victoria in east-central Africa is the world's third largest lake. Only Lake Superior in North America and the Caspian Sea are larger.

HUMAN GROUPS

"Now tell us about the people of Africa," Panchito said. "Are they all Negroes? Are there white people living here? Any Asians?"

"An intelligent question," said Donald. "One that I'd be most happy to answer."

"Please, Donald," José Carioca pleaded. "I want to hear all about those fierce cannibals."

"Cannibals!" Donald bellowed. And

A young Danakil woman. The Danakils live in the desert areas of Ethiopia. They are mostly shepherds and farmers.
Facing: Winnowing teff, a cereal grass which grows in the dry regions of Ethiopia.

for the first time in the trip he was very angry. "There are no cannibals in Africa. Forget all those stupid adventure books you've been reading and the Tarzan movies you've been seeing."

He glared again at Carioca and then went on in a calmer tone. "To answer Panchito. There are two major groups on the continent: the Negroid and the Caucasoid. Negroes are by far the largest population group. There are over 200,000,000 Negroes in Africa. They live in most of the continent, except for northern Africa. Some of the Negroes, especially the Watusi, or Tutsi, of east-central Africa, are very tall—sometimes over 7 feet. The pygmies of tropical central Africa are among the shortest peoples in the world.

Above and right: Rubber trees growing in one of the forests of the Ivory Coast, a country of West Africa.

Left: Ethiopian women harvesting sugarcane. Some scholars believe that sugarcane was first cultivated in tropical Africa. Today the plant is grown in most of the warm areas of the world.

Another short people, the Bushmen, are found mostly in the Kalahari Desert region of southwestern Africa.

More Caucasians than Negroes live in North Africa, the part of the continent north of the Sahara. There are some 75,000,000 Arabs and Berbers living in that region. A large number of Caucasians from Europe have settled in southern Africa. In the Republic of South Africa, for example, there are more than 3,500,-000 people of European descent. There are close to 1,000,000 Asians in Africa who are also Caucasians.

NORTHERN AFRICA

And now, we'll take a quick survey of the continent, region by region. I'll name the countries and tell you something about them. In order to make things clear we'll divide Africa into three regions: The northern, central, and southern. Okay? Now let's be on our way.

Harvesting and sorting cotton in Egypt. Cotton is the country's most important crop. The art of growing and processing cotton is very old and sprang up in different parts of the world. Some historians believe that cotton was first grown in India.

The northern region is made up of Mauritania, Spanish Sahara, Morocco, Algeria, Libya, Egypt, Tunisia, Mali, Niger, Chad and Sudan. For a great many years most of this region has been a food-producing area. Dates, olives, and grapes are grown, along with vegetables and cereals. The grazing lands are used for sheep, goats and cattle, whose wool and hides are exported. There is some mining of metals in some parts of North Africa. The large deposits of oil discovered in Algeria and Libya have made these two countries important oil producers. Egypt has built one of the world's greatest dams, the Aswan High Dam. It is expected to double the nation's power capacity.

"In most of these countries a large part of the people are Arab. The Muslim religion is followed by many of the people. Arabic and French are the main languages. All of the countries are independent except for Spanish Sahara, which is an overseas province of Spain.

Above: The soil of a section of the Danakil plains in Ethiopia. The striking colors of the earth are due to the impure iron particles mixed with the sand.
Below: A street in Niamey, capital of Niger.
Opposite page: A copper mine in Zaire. In the foreground, lined up like stone slabs, are blocks of copper.

a

b

c

d

e

Two major groups of people live in Africa, the Negroid and the Caucasoid. Negroes are by far the largest population group of the continent. There are more than 250,000,000 Negroes in Africa. They usually have dark brown hair and skin and may be divided into many subgroups. Negroes occupy most of Africa, with the exception of northern Africa. In the northern portions of western Africa and in many parts of eastern Africa most of the people are of mixed Negro and Caucasian stock. North Africa has two major subgroups of Caucasians, the Arabs and the Berbers. They total some 75,000,000 people. Both groups are Muslims (followers of the Muslim religion). A large number of Caucasians from Europe have settled in southern Africa. The Republic of South Africa has more than 3,500,000 people of European descent.

Some peoples of Africa.
a) Arab Boy (Egypt)
b) Somali youth
c) Young girl (Ethiopia)
d) Berber maiden (Morocco)
e) Pygmy from Zaire
f) Baluba from Zaire
g) Woman from the
   Malagasy Republic
h) Man from Kenya
i) Afrikaner child (South
   Africa)

Opposite page: A group of Watusi, or Tutsi, from Burundi. They are very tall people, many of them over 7 feet.

g

h

i

86

*Above: Kariba Dam on the Zambezi River, which
forms the border of Rhodesia and Zambia.
Left: Johannesburg, gold center of South Africa.*

CENTRAL AFRICA

Now, let's go into central Africa. There are three countries with the name of Guinea. So pay close attention."

"Three?" asked José Carioca. "Then how in the world does one tell the difference between them?"

"A good question," nodded Panchito. "My friend José asks good questions."

"Nonsense! He doesn't," Donald snapped impatiently. "Anyway, there's a simple answer to this one. There are Portuguese Guinea, Equatorial Guinea, and just plain Guinea. Portuguese Guinea is an overseas province of Portugal. Equatorial Guinea, which used to be called Spanish Guinea, became an indepent country in 1968. Guinea, or the Republic of Guinea, was a French colony. It became independent in 1958. And while we're on the subject of independence, listen to this. Before World War II there

Above: Khartoum, capital of Sudan.
Right: Top photograph is a view of Algiers.
Right: Modern Tunis.

were only four independent countries in Africa. Today there are 43 such countries in the continent and its adjoining islands.

Now for the rest of the countries in central Africa. They are Senegal, The Gambia, Sierra Leone, Liberia, Ivory Coast, Ghana, Togo, Dahomey, Upper Volta, Nigeria, Cameroon, Central African Republic, Ethiopia, Somalia, Gabon, Congo (Brazzaville), Zaire, Uganda, Burundi, Kenya, and Tanzania.

There is one thing that many of these countries have in common. Their governments are doing their best to improve the lot of their peoples. They are trying to move them into the 20th-century world of science and technology. Zaire and Gabon have large mineral deposits. Nigeria has an adequate supply of tin and is one of the few countries in Africa that mines coal.

Liberia is the oldest republic in Africa. It was founded early in the 19th century as a home for freed American slaves. Ethiopia, a constitutional monarchy, is the oldest independent country in Africa.

SOUTHERN AFRICA

The countries of southern Africa are: Angola, Zambia, Malawi, Mozambique, South West Africa (Namibia), Rhodesia, Botswana. Lesotho, Swaziland, South Africa, Malagasy Republic, Mauritius.

All of the countries are independent except for Mozambique, South West Africa and Angola. Angola and Mozambique are overseas provinces of Portugal. South West Africa (Namibia) is claimed by two powers: South Africa and the United Nations. Rhodesia has declared itself a republic but the United Nations has refused to recognize it.

"And now," said Donald. "We shall leave Africa. Dumbo, fly us east. Next stop Australia, please."

THE FABLED LANDS

Dumbo raised his huge ears. Flap, flap, —higher and higher they all went into the shining blue sky. Donald settled himself into a soft spot and looked down on the huge body of water underneath.

"Don't get tired, Dumbo, because there's no place to rest down there."

"We're going over the Indian Ocean," Panchito said.

José Carioca had nothing to say, for he was sound asleep. And so the hours passed. Finally, Dumbo began flying lower and lower, and then suddenly Donald and Panchito saw the coast of Australia loom up before them.

"Wake up, José," they cried.

"We're here," said Dumbo proudly.

And the instant they landed they saw their first kangaroo. He was standing on the beach, staring at them. Donald went over to him, bowed and said:

"We've come to be guests of your great and fabulous land."

The kangaroo hopped away.

"Well," said Donald quietly. "I never

A baby platypus. At birth these little creatures are only about 1 inch long. The platypus is found only in Australia.

expected such behavior from a marsupial."

And before Panchito could ask him what a marsupial was, Donald had whipped out his trusty encyclopedia.

"Marsupials are animals that produce small, immature offspring that are carried in the mother's pouch until the babies are fully developed. Nearly half of Australia's native mammals are marsupials, and the kangaroos are the most famous of all."

And then he turned and looked in the direction of the vanished kangaroo and said:

"And have the worst manners of all!"

They all sat on the wide beach and looked out over the greenish water to the distant, shining horizon.

"Donald," said José Carioca, "You called this a fabulous land. Why?"

"Well," said Donald—and this time he did not have to consult the encyclopedia, for while they were sleeping he had read a short history of Australia—"well, in the 13th century Marco Polo, the famous explorer and trader, spoke of a kingdom which was located in the south. It was a land rich in spices and treasure—a fabulous

land. It is almost certain that he was talking of a land south of Sumatra. But the people of his day thought he meant an area way south of the equator. This started a search for the fabulous *terra australis incognita*, or "the unknown southern land."

"And so began a period of great explorations by men such as Ferdinand Magellan, Abel Janszoon Tasman, and Captain James Cook. It was Cook who in 1770 was able to explore a good part of the continent. But he never went into the interior of Australia. It was only in the last century that this area was first ex-

Left: The iron bridge that joins the two sections of Sydney, the capital of New South Wales. Sydney is Australia's oldest and largest city and the country's chief industrial and commercial center.

Above: Modern buildings in Canberra, the capital city of Australia.
Below: A view of a mining city in Queensland.

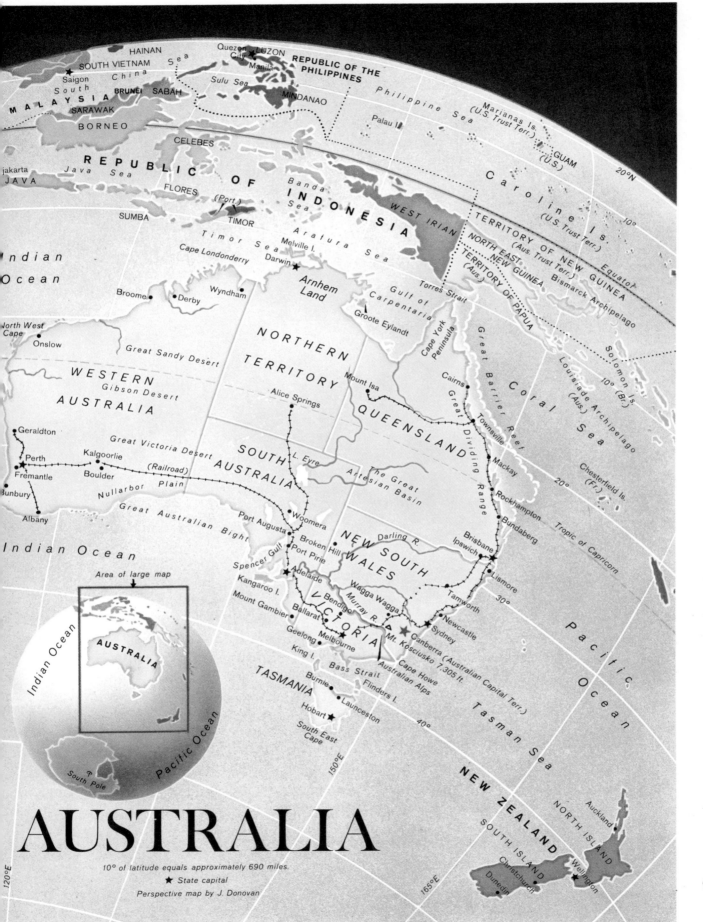

HAINAN
SOUTH VIETNAM
Saigon
MALAYSIA
BRUNEI SABAH
SARAWAK
BORNEO

China Sea
South

Quezon City ★LUZON **REPUBLIC OF THE PHILIPPINES**
Manila
Sulu Sea
MINDANAO

Philippine Sea

Marianas Is.
(U.S. Trust Terr.)
GUAM
(U.S.)

20°N

Palau Is.

Caroline Is.
(U.S. Trust Terr.)

10°

Jakarta
JAVA
Java Sea
FLORES
SUMBA
TIMOR
(Port.)

R E P U B L I C   O F   I N D O N E S I A
Banda Sea
WEST IRIAN

TERRITORY OF NEW GUINEA
(Aus. Trust Terr.)
NORTH EAST NEW GUINEA
(Aus.)
TERRITORY OF PAPUA
(Aus.)

Equator

Bismarck Archipelago

10°

Indian Ocean

Cape Londonderry
Melville I.
Darwin ★
Arnhem Land

Timor Sea
Arafura Sea

Gulf of Carpentaria

Torres Strait

Solomon Is.
10° (Br.)

Louisiade Archipelago
(Aus.)

North West Cape
Onslow
Broome
Derby
Wyndham

Groote Eylandt

Cape York Peninsula

Cairns

Great Barrier Reef

C o r a l   S e a

Chesterfield Is.
(Fr.)

20°

Great Sandy Desert

N O R T H E R N   T E R R I T O R Y

Mount Isa

Townsville

Great Dividing Range

W E S T E R N
Gibson Desert
A U S T R A L I A

Alice Springs

Q U E E N S L A N D

Mackay

Geraldton
Perth
Kalgoorlie
Fremantle
Boulder
Bunbury
Albany

Great Victoria Desert

**S O U T H
A U S T R A L I A**

L. Eyre

The Great Artesian Basin

Rockhampton
Bundaberg

Tropic of Capricorn

(Railroad)
Nullarbor   Plain

Great Australian Bight

Woomera
Port Augusta
Broken Hill
Port Pirie
Spencer Gulf
Kangaroo I.

**N E W   S O U T H
W A L E S**

Darling R.

Brisbane
Ipswich

Lismore

Pacific

30°

Area of large map

Adelaide ★

Mount Gambier
Ballarat

AUSTRALIA

Wagga Wagga

Tamworth

Indian Ocean

Bendigo
Geelong
Melbourne
King I.

V I C T O R I A

Murray R.
Canberra (Australian Capital Terr.)
Cape Howe
Mt. Kosciusko 7,305 ft.
Australian Alps

Newcastle
Sydney

Ocean

South Pole

Pacific Ocean

T A S M A N I A
Burnie
Hobart ★
Launceston
Flinders I.

Bass Strait

Tasman Sea

40°

South East Cape

150°E

120°E

AUSTRALIA

10° of latitude equals approximately 690 miles.
★ State capital
Perspective map by J. Donovan

165°E

N E W   Z E A L A N D

Auckland
NORTH ISLAND
SOUTH ISLAND
Christchurch
Wellington
Dunedin

plored. So you can see how new a world Australia really is."

They were silent for a while, listening to the steady sound of the huge waves as they broke upon the beach.

"Do you know," Donald said, "that this is what the weather is like at Christmas. Sunny and hot."

"At Christmas? You mean no snow, no sleighriding, no crackling fireplaces?"

"Exactly!" Donald nodded. "Since Australia lies in the Southern Hemisphere, winter comes in July and summer in December. So the Australian school children flock to the beaches to swim and play all during their Christmas vacations. And thinking of the ocean makes me think of water. For Australia is the driest of all the continents—most parts of

Australia do not get enough rainfall. In some places there is a severe drought every single year. In other places there are droughts, but not that often. Much of inland Australia is desert—gray, barren, and uninhabited.

THE SURVIVORS

At that moment the kangaroo appeared again. He hopped up to the group, smiled at Panchito and José Carioca but looked coldly at Donald and hopped away again.

"Manners, manners," said Donald angrily. "Now a koala would never do a thing like that."

"A koala?"

"Yes," said Donald. "He too is a marsupial. But he's lovable and is loved. He looks like a child's teddy bear and spends his day curled up in an eucalyptus tree. The koala drinks no water but lives entirely on the leaves of these trees.

"Because Australia is isolated from the rest of the world—it is an island continent —animals like the marsupials have survived from prehistoric times. For example, there is the platypus, a very strange creature indeed. He has four webbed feet and a long snout shaped like a duck's bill. Australia has many strange birds. The emu, the continent's largest bird, cannot fly but is a fast runner. Then there is the lyrebird. He's some mimic. He can sing more than 40 different birdcalls. What do you think of that!

THE ABORIGINES

"The aborigines were the first inhabitants of Australia. It is believed that they came to the continent some 20,000 to 30,000 years ago. Up till two centuries ago they had no contact with the outside world. They were nomads who fished and

Tropical fish swim between the branches of a coral in New Caledonia. Coral is found in warm, semitropical, and tropical seas.

hunted. They had no agriculture. The dingo, a dog found in Australia to this day, was their only domestic animal. The aborigines are slowly adapting themselves to the Australia of today.

AUSTRALIA—THE COMMONWEALTH

"The Commonwealth of Australia is made up of six states. Five are on the mainland—New South Wales, Victoria, Queensland, South Australia, and Western Australia. The sixth is the island state of Tasmania.

"There are also two territories on the mainland. In the north is the large Northern Territory. In the southeast is the small Australian Capital Territory in which is Canberra, the capital of Australia. The other major cities are Sydney, Melbourne, Adelaide, Perth, and Brisbane. About 80 percent of the population live in cities.

"Australia is the earth's smallest continent and largest island. It is the only continent occupied by a single nation. It has a population of some 12,550,000 and is an English-speaking nation. Since World War II about 2,000,000 new settlers have come to Australia from other parts of the world. Some of them have settled on the vast grasslands where sheep are raised. Wool is the country's single most important export item." "Any other countries in that area?" asked José Carioca.

"Well, there is New Zealand, about 1,200 miles away in the South Pacific Ocean. New Zealand is made up of two islands. And then there's icy Antarctica, where penguins live. We'll fly over it on our way home."

95

THE NEW WORLD

During the short flight that was to take our travelers from the South Pole to the New World, Donald never lifted his eyes from his encyclopedia. He was too busy gathering information to say a word. After all, the New World was his home and he did not want his friends to discover that there were questions for which he might not have a quick answer.

As a result of his studying, Donald was bursting with facts when he saw the lights of a town twinkling at the tip of South America.

"Look," he shouted to his friends. "There is Ushuaia, the southernmost town in the world. It is on one of the islands of Tierra del Fuego. This group of islands is separated from the South American mainland by the Strait of Magellan. The islands were given their name, which means "Land of Fire" in Spanish, by the great navigator Magellan in 1520 when he saw campfires burning there."

The Statue of Liberty, a gift to the United States from France, is the first greeting to people coming to the New World.

"Hey, wait a minute, Donald," called José Carioca. "We're about to set foot in South America. Isn't that more important than Magellan and campfires?"

Donald looked a little surprised at this interruption, but he had to admit that José Carioca was right. He still wanted to tell his friends all he had learned, however, so he immediately continued his lecture.

"Do you know what year Europeans first set foot on South America?" Donald asked.

"Oh, that's easy," replied Panchito and José Carioca almost in one voice. "The year was 1492."

"You're absolutely wrong," Donald said to them in his best schoolteacher manner.

"Columbus did not reach South America until his third voyage to the New World in 1498. On that trip he reached the mouth of the Orinoco River in Venezuela."

Both José Carioca and Panchito now looked properly embarrassed. They did not seem ready to interrupt again, so Donald went on happily with his speech.

Above: Skyscrapers soar over Park Avenue in New York City, which is known for its very tall buildings. Opposite page: Another kind of skyscraper—oil wells in Venezuela, one of the world's leading petroleum-producing nations.

99

Two views of the southwestern
United States.
Above: Navaho Indian children
on a reservation in Arizona.
Opposite page: A traditional
Indian pueblo in New Mexico.

"South America is the fourth largest continent. It is shaped like a triangle with its wide base in the north and its narrow tip in the south. South America is home to almost 185,000,000 people. The main languages are Spanish and Portuguese. Portuguese is spoken in Brazil.

"The continent of South America is surrounded on all sides by water," Donald continued.

"And it extends farther into the Antarctic regions than any other inhabited land," interrupted José Carioca who could not keep such an exciting piece of information to himself.

"Right, José," said Donald, "But did you know that South America has few good natural harbors because the coast is so even? And did you know that there are only two South American countries that do not border the sea?

"Sure, I knew that, Donald. They are Bolivia and Paraguay." And he couldn't resist adding a small triumphant "ha!" at the end of his sentence.

Our friend Donald was still full of facts. "The nations of Colombia, Venezuela, Guyana, Surinam, French Guiana, Brazil, Uruguay, and Argentina border the sea on the north and east coast of

A view of British Columbia, in western Canada. Canada is the second largest nation in the world after the Soviet Union. Top of page: Coffee beans drying in Ecuador.

Above: Donald Duck bravely takes a look at the Grand Canyon of the Colorado River in Arizona, shown in facing photograph. The 217-mile-long canyon is one of the great natural wonders of the United States.

South America. Chile, Peru, and Ecuador open onto the Pacific coast.

"Some of the South American countries also have island possessions in the seas that touch their shores. The Galápagos Islands in the Pacific belong to Ecuador, and the Juan Fernández Islands, also in the Pacific, belong to Chile. The Falkland Islands in the Pacific are a dependency of the United Kingdom, but Argentina claims the Falklands and calls them the Islas Malvinas.

"What about the weather in South America?" asked Panchito, who started shivering when he even thought about the South Pole.

Donald was, as usual, completely ready with an answer. "Panchito, you have your

choice of climates in South America because the landscape is so full of variety. At the peak of the Andes, the highest mountains in the Western Hemisphere, you will find snow the year round. The weather is very hot and humid in the basin of the Amazon River, which is surrounded by the largest rain forest in the world. The other extreme is Chile's Atacama Desert, where there is so little rain that it cannot be measured. The umbrella business is very bad there.

Loyal citizen of South America that he was, José Carioca had tried more than once to dam up the flood of information pouring from Donald's beak. And now, when Donald stopped for a moment to catch his breath, José saw that his moment

Top, right: The jagged Atlantic coastline of Canada's Nova Scotia peninsula. The coastal waters off this part of Canada, especially the Bay of Fundy, have extremely strong tides. Lower right: Wintertime near the city of Quebec.

had come. He puffed up his feathers and started to talk.

"Okay, Donald, enough. Nobody knows better than I do how beautiful and varied South America is. It is I who have sailed in a boat across Lake Titicaca, the world's highest lake, and it is I who have skied in the Chilean Alps. It was I, not you, who rode with the gauchos—the Argentine cowboys—to guide the cattle on the pampas, or grassy plain, as you would call it. But you say nothing of the wonderful South American people, of their cities, their music and dances, or the things they make with their hands and in their factories." José was quiet for a moment. His speech had been so exciting to make that he had to rest for a bit.

Donald, you will not be surprised to learn, was a little bit ashamed but he could not stop talking. He just changed to the topic José Carioca had suggested.

PEOPLE, PLACES, AND PRODUCTS OF SOUTH AMERICA

"Err, hhmm, yes, José. The first people to make their home in South America were Indians," Donald began and José Carioca nodded his head in agreement.

"Next came the Europeans, the Spanish and their neighbors the Portuguese, who settled mainly in Brazil. Negroes, who were first brought to South America as 105

slaves, make up the third large group. All three groups—the Indians, Europeans, and Negroes—have intermarried and there is a good deal of racial harmony in Latin America.

Over 90 percent of the South Americans are Roman Catholics, as were the first European settlers. In the more remote areas of the land, Indians mix their ancient rituals with Catholicism.

"The most important products of these varied people and their varied land," Donald went on, "come from farms and mines."

"Amazingly, although only about 5 percent of South America is devoted to farmland, the different climates make it possible to grow all kinds of crops. Corn is the most important food and coffee and sugar are the leading exports. In the highlands of the Andes potatoes and barley

Opposite page: Monument Valley in Arizona. Below: The Andes seen from the air. Right: Niagara Falls, on the United States–Canadian border, are the highest falls in North America.

Above: A glacial valley in the Canadian Rockies. The marks on the rocks show that the glacier has moved across this region. Opposite page: The coconut harvest in Nicaragua, the largest nation in Central America.

are grown, but along the tropical coasts it is possible to raise coconuts, citrus fruits, and bananas. Beef cattle are raised in many places—Argentina, Uruguay, southern Brazil, and Venezuela.

"Don't forget the mines," José Carioca reminded Donald.

"I won't," Donald answered. "Mining ranks as South America's second most important industry after farming. You remember how excited the Spanish explorers were by the mineral riches of South America? Even today every South American country except Paraguay and Uruguay can claim to mine some minerals such as gold, silver, lead, zinc, copper, and oil. And in different countries there are deposits of tin, bauxite, iron, platinum, emeralds, diamonds, and semiprecious stones. Venezuela is the third largest oil-producing country in the world, and Brazil has about a quarter of the world's iron reserves. As you would guess, the products of South America's mines and farms are its most important exports.

"And now, José Carioca, don't be impatient. We will fly quickly from one great city to another. Let us stop first at Brazil's brand new capital, Brasília. Wait until you see its marvelous modern buildings. Then we can fly low over São Paulo, the bustling industrial center of Brazil. Then we'll go south to the beautiful old city of Rio de Janeiro, which used to be Brazil's capital. We'll fly south again to Buenos Aires, capital of Argentina. It is one of the handsomest cities in the world with its broad avenues and impressive monuments. We cannot leave South America without a visit to Lima, Peru's capital and once the richest and most important Spanish city on the continent. On to busy modern Caracas in Venezuela. And then off we go to the lovely lands of Central America.

STEPPING-STONES IN THE CARIBBEAN SEA

José Carioca was growing fidgety again. "Hey, Donald," he asked, "Are we going to North America by way of the island stepping-stones in the Caribbean Sea or by way of Central America?"

Donald scratched his head for a minute, then whispered something to Dumbo, and finally answered José Carioca, who was impatiently tapping his foot.

"Dumbo and I," Donald announced seriously, "think it would be more fun to fly from Venezuela across the islands of the Caribbean and then go to the mainland of Central America to see what we can see. Is that Okay with you?"

"Dandy!" agreed José and Panchito.

Donald, of course, started lecturing at

This is the view our four heroes had of Buenos Aires, Argentina, one of the world's loveliest cities.

WEST INDIES
CUBA
DOMINICAN REPUBLIC
JAMAICA HAITI PUERTO RICO GUADELOUPE (Fr.)
(U.S.)
Caribbean Sea BARBADOS (Br.)
CENTRAL Panama Canal Barranquilla TRINIDAD AND TOBAGO (Br.)
AMERICA Maracaibo Caracas ★
10°N PANAMA VENEZUELA GUYANA
Medellín Georgetown ★ Paramaribo
COCOS IS. ★ Bogotá SURINAM ★ Cayenne
(C.R.) COLOMBIA FR. GUIANA
MALPELO IS.
(Col.) Cali Manaus Belém
Equator Quito ★ •
ECUADOR Guayaquil Equator 0°
GALÁPAGOS IS.
(Ecua.) Fortaleza

PERU BRAZIL Recife
10°S Callao Lima 10°S
• Cuzco
L. BOLIVIA Brasília ★ Salvador
Pacific Titicaca La Paz ★
• Sucre Belo Horizonte
Ocean •
PARAGUAY Rio de Janeiro
20°S Asunción São Paulo • 20°S
Tropic of Capricorn Santos Tropic of Capricorn

SAN FÉLIX IS. Pôrto Alegre
(Chile) SAN AMBROSIO IS.
(Chile) South
ARGENTINA
• Córdoba Atlantic
Rosario • URUGUAY
30°S Ocean 30°S
JUAN FERNÁNDEZ ISLANDS Santiago Buenos Aires ★ Montevideo
(Chile) Valparaíso Río de la Plata

Concepción

Bahía Blanca

SOUTH
40°S CHILOÉ IS. 40°S
AMERICA

Taitao Pen.

Perspective map by J. Donovan

Strait of FALKLAND ISLANDS
Magellan ISLAS MALVINAS
(Br., claimed by Arg.)
Punta Arenas • SOUTH GEORGIA
50°S TIERRA DEL FUEGO (Br.) 50°S
Cape Horn
90°W 75°W 60°W 45°W 30°W

North
Atlantic
Ocean
20°N
Tropic of Cancer
10°N

once. "Below us is the blue Caribbean Sea, which takes its name from the Carib Indians who once lived there. The sea is an important waterway because it is linked with the Pacific by way of the Panama Canal.

"The several hundred islands in the sea are divided into two groups—the Greater Antilles and the Lesser Antilles. The four biggest islands are in the Greater Antilles. They are Cuba, Hispaniola (divided between Haiti and the Dominican Republic), Jamaica, and Puerto Rico. Columbus landed at Hispaniola in 1492," Donald added, looking directly at José Carioca, "during his first voyage to the New World.

"Cuba, Haiti, Jamaica, and the Dominican Republic are independent nations. Puerto Rico is a commonwealth within the United States.

"The Lesser Antilles are divided into two groups—the Leeward Islands, which include the United States' Virgin Islands, and the Windward Islands, which include Trinidad and Tobago.

"I wish we could stay in the Caribbean region a little longer," Donald added. The climate and the beaches are great. Lots of people seem to agree, because tourists provide the islanders with a major part of their income."

THE CENTRAL AMERICAN LAND BRIDGE

Our tireless travelers then headed for Central America, which is a land bridge linking North and South America. Before our heroes touch down, we'll quickly review the names of the Central American nations. They are British Honduras (also known as Belize), Guatemala, Honduras, El Salvador, Nicaragua, Costa Rica, Pan-

A steel plant in Concepción, in south central Chile, a major mineral-producing nation.

112

ama, and the Panama Canal Zone. All these countries except the Panama Canal Zone and British Honduras are independent republics that were once Spanish colonies, and Spanish is still the major language. In British Honduras, English is the chief language.

But let's get back to our flying friends. Donald was talking again. "Central America has a backbone of mountains—a link between the Andes of South America and the Rockies of North America. Because of the many volcanoes in the region the soil has been enriched with lava and ash. Today the Central Americans export large quantities of coffee as well as bananas, cotton, and lumber from their dense tropical forests. It would be fun to stay longer to explore these sun-drenched countries, but we still have the whole

Sand being filtered in a diamond mine in the state of Rio Branco, Brazil.

Day and night, a never-ending stream of ships passes through Miraflores Locks in the Panama Canal.

113

enormous expanse of North America to visit before we head back to Disneyland."

THE THREE NATIONS OF NORTH AMERICA

"Geographers often include Central America as part of the North American continent," Donald said, "but we are going to do it a little differently. For one short tour North America will include only three nations—Mexico, Canada, and last but hardly least, the United States."

"And here," said Panchito courageously, "it is my turn to talk because as we climb to the north the first country we meet is MY Mexico."

Donald looked a little surprised at this outburst, but he nodded his head and said, "Go ahead, Panchito."

"My Mexico," Panchito said, "is a land of dramatic contrasts. It has high mountains, burning deserts, steaming jungles, and fine cities, old ones and new ones.

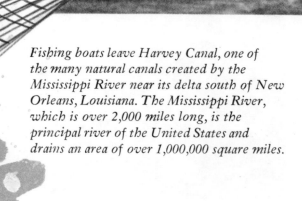

Fishing boats leave Harvey Canal, one of the many natural canals created by the Mississippi River near its delta south of New Orleans, Louisiana. The Mississippi River, which is over 2,000 miles long, is the principal river of the United States and drains an area of over 1,000,000 square miles.

"The Mexican people are descended from the original Indian settlers and from the Spanish who settled in Mexico centuries ago. Most Mexicans are Roman Catholics and the main language is Spanish, although many Indians still speak their native dialects.

"Mexico can be divided into five main regions. The long, narrow peninsula of Baja California (Lower California) is separated from the mainland by the Gulf of California. It is a region of high mountains in the east and desert elsewhere. The second geographical division is made up of the major mountains—the Sierra Madre Oriental and the Sierra Madre Occidental.

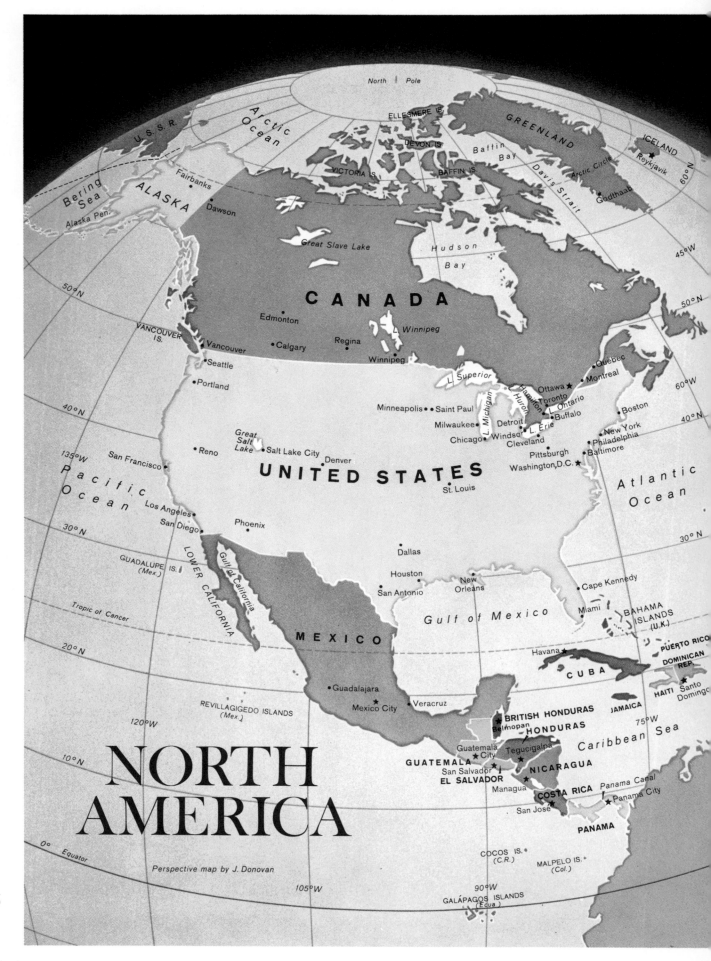

North | Pole

Arctic Ocean

U.S.S.R.

ELLESMERE IS.

GREENLAND

ICELAND

Reykjavik

DEVON IS.

Baffin Bay

60°N

VICTORIA IS.

BAFFIN IS.

Arctic Circle

Godthaab

45°W

Fairbanks

ALASKA

Bering Sea

Dawson

Alaska Pen.

Great Slave Lake

Hudson Bay

50°N

CANADA

Edmonton

L. Winnipeg

Quebec

Montreal

VANCOUVER IS.

Vancouver

Calgary

Regina

Winnipeg

L. Superior

Ottawa

Toronto

Ontario

60°N

50°N

Seattle

Hamilton

L. Huron

Boston

Portland

40°N

Minneapolis

Saint Paul

L. Michigan

Buffalo

New York

135°W

San Francisco

Milwaukee

Detroit

L. Erie

Philadelphia

40°N

Reno

Great Salt Lake

Salt Lake City

Chicago

Windsor

Cleveland

Pittsburgh

Baltimore

Denver

Washington,D.C.

Pacific Ocean

UNITED STATES

St. Louis

Atlantic Ocean

Los Angeles

Phoenix

30°N

San Diego

Dallas

30°N

GUADALUPE IS. (Mex.)

LOWER CALIFORNIA

Gulf of California

Houston

New Orleans

Cape Kennedy

Tropic of Cancer

San Antonio

Gulf of Mexico

Miami

BAHAMA ISLANDS (U.K.)

20°N

MEXICO

PUERTO RICO

Havana

DOMINICAN REP.

CUBA

HAITI

Santo Domingo

120°W

Guadalajara

JAMAICA

75°W

REVILLAGIGEDO ISLANDS (Mex.)

Mexico City

Veracruz

BRITISH HONDURAS

Belmopan

HONDURAS

10°N

Guatemala City

Tegucigalpa

Caribbean Sea

GUATEMALA

San Salvador

NICARAGUA

EL SALVADOR

Managua

Panama Canal

NORTH AMERICA

COSTA RICA

Panama City

San José

PANAMA

0°   Equator

COCOS IS. (C.R.)

MALPELO IS. (Col.)

Perspective map by J. Donovan

105°W

90°W

GALÁPAGOS ISLANDS (Ecua.)

They join to form a magnificent mountain area in central Mexico. Between the two Sierra ranges lies a third region, the Central Plateau, where two thirds of the population lives. A fourth type of region, coastal plains, is located along the coasts of the Gulf of California and the coasts of the Gulf of Mexico. Finally we come to the Yucatan Peninsula, which is a huge limestone plain that is wooded in spots and covered by jungle and swamps elsewhere.

"The climate of Mexico depends on which of the geographical regions you are visiting and how high above sea level you are. In Mexico, as elsewhere, the higher you go the cooler you will be!

"Farming, livestock raising, fishing, and forestry are the most important parts of the Mexican economy. The minerals that attracted the Spanish are still important too. They include sulfur, iron, copper, zinc, and silver. The most important industry is textile manufacturing.

"Although almost half of the Mexican people still live outside the great cities, no visit to Mexico is complete without a tour of the capital, Mexico City. Built on the site of the Aztec Indian city of Tenochtitlán by the Spaniards, Mexico City is today an exciting blend of yesterday and today. Its population of over 6 million makes it Mexico's largest city. Other important cities are Tampico, Guadalajara, Oaxaca, Villahermosa, and Mérida.

"Thank you, Panchito," Donald interrupted, "but we must fly to Canada now."

"Canada," Donald began in his lecture voice, "is the largest nation in the Western Hemisphere and the second largest nation in the world after the Soviet Union. It is a self-governing confederation within the British Commonwealth of Nations and is made up of 10 provinces and two territories.

"The Canadian people are mainly of British and French origin and both English and French are used for government business. Other important Canadian population groups are the Indians and the Eskimos.

"You should not be surprised to find that Canada's great size has given it a rich variety of landscapes. They include the rolling hills of the Appalachian highlands and the plains of the Great Lakes–St. Lawrence River region. The scenery varies dramatically from the barren but mineral-rich Canadian Shield in the north to the endless sweep of the interior plains. The landscape changes again in the west with the towering beauty of the Canadian Rockies. Because of the cold of its northlands, only a narrow band of this vast nation, the area along the United States–Canadian border, is densely settled.

Canada's climate is also varied. In general, winters are long and cold, summers are short and mild. However, Canada's transportation resources—its rivers and lakes—and its great natural wealth have formed the basis of a thriving economy. The country's natural resources include its vast forests, the fish of its lakes, rivers, and seas, and a variety of minerals including petroleum, copper, uranium, iron ore, gold, zinc, lead, silver and nickel.

"Canada's most important industries are farming, lumbering, and mining. The centers of banking, industry, and government are the great cities of the east: Ottawa, the capital city; Toronto, Montreal, and Quebec. The largest city in the west is Vancouver.

"And now," said Donald, "it is time to tour my country, the United States of America, or as the poets call it, "America the Beautiful."

"The United States," Donald said in a voice full of pride, "is the fourth largest nation in the world. Only the Soviet

Union, Canada, and China are larger. It is also one of the richest and most varied lands on the globe. However, in our short tour we will only be able to describe the highlights.

"Geographers say the mainland United States of America can be divided into three major regions—the eastern highlands, the large central plains region, and the great mountains of the west, including the Rockies. The Rockies are the northern continuation of the mountain chain that we saw first as the Andes in South America.

"The two youngest states—Alaska and Hawaii—are unique. Alaska, the most northerly state, includes the Aleutian Islands, one of the longest volcanic island chains in the world. Hawaii, the first island state, is over 2,000 miles from the mainland. Hawaii is actually made up of many mountainous islands, some of which still have active volcanoes.

"Like Canada, the United States is very rich in lakes, rivers, and natural resources. All of these have helped to make the country prosperous. The most famous river is the Mississippi, which drains the central region. Much of the land is dotted with large and small lakes. The biggest are the Great Lakes, which lie along or near the border of Canada. Their names are Huron, Ontario, Michigan, Erie, and Superior. Notice that combining the first letters of each lake spells HOMES. Superior is the world's second largest lake—after the Caspian Sea.

"The United States has such a wealth of mineral resources there isn't time to tell you about all of them. It has over one third of the world's coal reserves. It is the world's leading producer of oil and natural gas, and is one of the world's leading iron producers. Copper, lead, zinc, silver, tungsten, phosphate, gold, and mercury

are also found. You shouldn't be surprised then to discover that the United States is the world's leading manufacturing nation. Its chief products are food and food products from its farms followed by transportation equipment, chemicals, and metal products and machinery.

"The population of the United States is over 200 million and is made up of people from all of the world's races and nations. Although you can hear nearly all of the world's languages spoken here, English is the nation's official language.

"More than two thirds of the population now lives in cities. The five largest are New York City—the biggest of them all—Chicago, Los Angeles, Philadelphia, and Detroit. The capital city, Washington, is not part of any state. It occupies a separate federal area called the District of Columbia.

"Where are we now?" asked Panchito

A fish-eye view of Disney World in Florida, which was opened to the public in 1971.